# INDEX ON CENSORSHIP

### A VOICE FOR THE PERSECUTED

VOL.53 // NO.2

SUMMER 2024

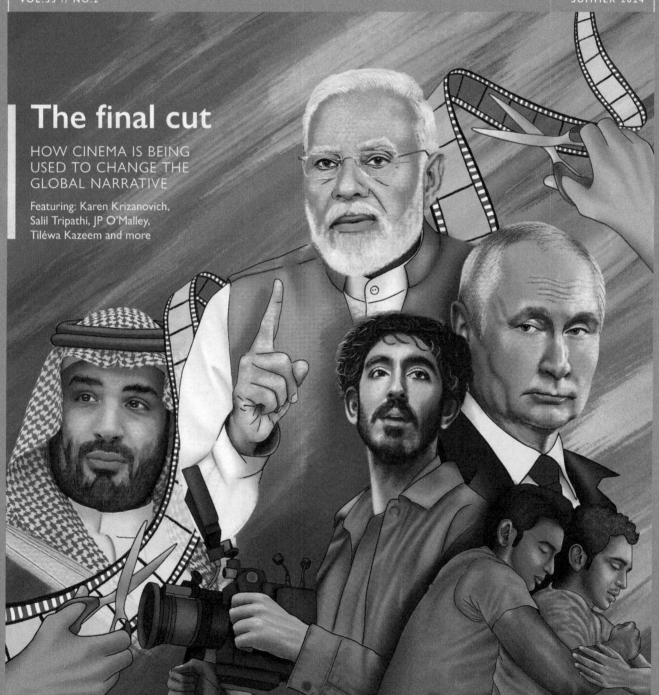

## The final cut

### HOW CINEMA IS BEING USED TO CHANGE THE GLOBAL NARRATIVE

Featuring: Karen Krizanovich, Salil Tripathi, JP O'Malley, Tiléwa Kazeem and more

**+ KATIE DANCEY-DOWNS**

A special Index investigation into book banning in UK schools

**+ CAN DÜNDAR**

Why exiled journalists must band together to challenge tyrants

**+ ANMOL IRFAN**

How mincels are learning from the Andrew Tate playbook

**+ NAZANIN ZAGHARI-RATCLIFFE**

The power of jailed rapper Toomaj Salehi's songs

INDEX ON CENSORSHIP
A VOICE FOR THE PERSECUTED

Thursday, 24 October 2024

# ANTI-SLAPP CONFERENCE

## Royal Irish Academy, Dublin

In association with

dri
Digital Repository of Ireland
Taisclann Dhigiteach na hÉireann

CASE
COALITION AGAINST SLAPPs IN EUROPE

UK Anti-SLAPP Coalition.

safety of journalists platform

Trinity College Dublin
Coláiste na Tríonóide, Baile Átha Cliath
The University of Dublin

## EDITOR'S LETTER

# Lights, camera, (red) - action

Index is going to the movies and exploring who determines what we see on screen, writes **Sally Gimson**

A S THE FIGHT for control of the global narrative rages on social media and in the dark corners of the internet, it is easy to forget that old 20th century phenomenon: film.

Movies are alive and kicking, and giant streaming sites are bringing them into our homes to watch whenever we feel the urge. Hollywood and US filmmakers still dominate the world stage and have a disproportionate influence on the global story. But as we discover in this issue there are plenty of governments keen to control what movie-watchers see and filmmakers

produce, not only in their own countries but across the world.

Saudi Arabia, as JP O'Malley and Mark Stimpson report, is pumping enormous sums of money into the international movie industry, paying Hollywood stars to come to their film festivals and building huge modern studios with the most up to date technology. Saudi Prince Mohammed Bin Salman (MBS) is clearly hoping that he can follow his success in sportswashing with filmwashing.

Meanwhile as author and expert Erich Schwartzel tells new CEO (and ex-Index editor-in-chief) Jemimah Steinfeld, China is also trying to make a splash in the movie world. It threw large sums into Hollywood blockbusters like Kung Fu Panda 3 and Mission: Impossible III, ensuring that these films gave a positive view of the Middle Kingdom. While some films paid for by China have been great successes, China has not really found its own movie-making groove. But with large investments in the Hollywood supply chains and an enormous domestic market, China's future ambitions to tell their story to the world should not be underestimated.

Over China's southern border in India, President Narendra Modi is allowing Hindu nationalists to bully Bollywood into censoring films which show Muslims in a moderate light. He's also encouraging filmmakers to make

movies which play into his nationalist playbook. Our South Asia editor Salil Tripathi has the story and remembers fondly when Bollywood reflected a more tolerant, religiously integrated India.

In our features section we have an exclusive investigation into censorship and school libraries in the UK. More than half of school librarians we surveyed said they had been asked to remove books and told us they had come under pressure from parents and some teachers to ban certain titles. The most disturbing part of the story is that one library service worker said she was not even offering books about LGBT+ issues to schools with large Muslim populations. I also worry that lots of librarians Index talked to were frightened to speak openly.

Look out for our short story by Kaya Genç about the most sensitive (read: censored) film in the world and some provocative pieces in our comment section including by award-winning Turkish journalist Can Dündar.

Finally, do read Jemimah's Global View. It gives you an idea of what she wants to do as chief executive. By the autumn, Index should also have a new editor. It's been a pleasure to work with our amazing team to see this magazine through to publication. ✖

*Sally Gimson is acting editor at Index*

53(02):1/1|DOI:10.1177/03064220241274921

## Blending pop culture and tradition

**Our cover has been inspired by traditional hand-painted Bollywood posters, an artform that is dying out**

AASTHA, WHO HAS designed our cover, is a Delhi-based visual artist. She has been crafting art since the age of five when she won a national painting competition. Her artistic journey has since been shaped by

her studies in English literature, art history, and motion graphics design, blending pop culture and traditional Indian elements to offer unique social commentary. Inspired by Mughal miniatures,

Rajasthani art and traditional paintings, her style combines historic references with modern flair. Aastha's characters embody the elegance, grace and stylisation of Bani Thani by Nihal Chand, a work

she deeply admires. Drawing inspiration from real women and conversations, her art reacts to the world around her, transforming themes and ideas into vibrant, thought-provoking pieces.

# CONTENTS

## Up Front

## Features

CREDIT: Lumli Lumlong

# The Index

53(02):4/10|DOI:10.1177/0306422024127032

A round-up of
events in the
world of free
expression
from Index's
unparalleled
network of
writers and
activists

Edited by
**MARK STIMPSON**

PICTURED: Iranian
director Mohammad
Rasoulof at the
2024 Cannes Film
Festival holds up
photos of actors
Soheila Golestani
(L) and Missagh
Zareh (R) from his
latest film The Seed
of the Sacred Fig.
Rasoulof fled over the
mountains to escape
imprisonment in Iran
just before the festival

## The Index

# ELECTION WATCH

The bumper election year continues. Here's who is heading to the polls next

LEFT TO RIGHT: Kais Saied is aiming to stifle dissent; Algeria's Abdelmadjid Tebboune; Filipe Nyusi expects to be re-elected

### 1. Tunisia

**EXPECTED SEPTEMBER OR OCTOBER 2024**

Tunisian president Kais Saied has spent his time in office dismantling democratic bodies and procedures in an attempt to consolidate his power. As the next election draws closer, Saied has increased his efforts to stifle dissent against his rule using Decree 54 – a law punishing the production and dissemination of "false news". This is widely seen as a crackdown on journalists, politicians and activists as he prepares to announce his candidacy for re-election. Three lawyers were arrested in May 2024 after criticising the Tunisian authorities. The country's main opposition organisation, the National Salvation Front, who campaigned heavily for the release of political prisoners jailed by Saied, have announced they will not stand in the next election due to it being an "electoral farce", suggesting more years of Saied in power are inevitable.

### 2. Algeria

**7 SEPTEMBER 2024**

Algeria's current president, Abdelmadjid Tebboune, is expected to run for re-election five years on from his victory in 2019, when turnout was just 58% due in part to boycotts by activists who were unhappy with the political system. The election comes three months earlier than expected. The military-backed leader has been accused by Amnesty International of creating a climate of fear by "escalating repression of peaceful dissent" during his first term in office. Algerian authorities have clamped down on dissenters, including members of the press, who criticise him. One such example is journalist Ihsane El Kadi, who was sentenced to five years in prison in 2023, a ruling condemned by the Committee to Protect Journalists. Tebboune will have to address such incidents during his campaign.

### 3. Mozambique

**9 OCTOBER 2024**

The last presidential election in Mozambique in 2019, which resulted in the re-election of President Filipe Nyusi of the dominant FRELIMO party, was widely accused of being corrupt. There were credible reports of tactics such as ballot stuffing and the intimidation of election officials, one of whom was even killed by 'elite police'. Municipal elections in 2023 suggest little has changed; FRELIMO secured a huge victory under similarly controversial circumstances, sparking protests from opposition supporters. The authorities responded brutally, with dozens arrested and at least four killed by a heavy-handed police response. In October, FRELIMO will once again be facing the electorate, this time with Daniel Chapo standing as their presidential candidate. If a similar pattern is followed, there is little doubt of the outcome. ✖

CREDIT: (Saied) Houcemmzoughi, (Tebboune) duma.gov.ru ,(Nyusi) Suzanne Plunkett

# World In Focus:
# Burkina Faso

**Burkina Faso was plunged into a state of chaos in 2022 by two military coups in the space of nine months, crippling free expression**

### 1 Ouagadougou

The state's current president is Captain Ibrahim Traoré, the leader of the military junta who ousted former ruler Lieutenant Colonel Paul-Henri Sandaogo Damiba, who had himself come to power by deposing the democratically elected president Roch Marc Christian Kaboré. These two successive military coups did nothing to improve the rights and freedoms of those in the country, as according to Freedom House military leaders further constrained the press. In 2022, authorities suspended French broadcaster Radio France Internationale for disseminating a message of intimidation attributed to a "terrorist leader", as well as expelling journalists working for French outlets Le Monde, Libération and France 24. Journalists in the region face significant threats such as being abducted or killed in militant attacks.

### 2 Pama reserve

Before the military coups, Burkina Faso was already a dangerous place for reporters because of the volatile security situation caused by militant groups, bandits and militias. In one particularly shocking incident in 2021, two Spanish journalists – documentary maker David Beriáin and cameraman Roberto Fraile - as well as Irish national Rory Young, director of the Chengeta Wildlife Foundation were killed when making an anti-poaching film. The government patrol convoy they were travelling in was ambushed by gunmen near Pama reserve. This tragedy bore similarities to the murder of French journalists Ghislaine Dupont and Claude Verlon in 2013, showing how little security conditions for press workers have improved over the years. While there remains no guarantee of safety from militant violence for reporters, a free press in Burkina Faso remains a very distant prospect.

### 3 Soro village massacre

In February 2024, the Burkina Faso military executed no fewer than 223 civilians accused of collaborating with Islamist armed groups in the deadliest army abuse the country has seen since 2015. The massacre occurred in Soro, a village in the Thiou district of the northern Yatenga province. At least 56 children were amongst those killed. Human Rights Watch - which broke the news with a report in April - was banned from the state afterwards, alongside foreign media organisations such as the UK's BBC and The Guardian, French outlets Le Monde and TV5Monde, Swiss broadcaster Agence Ecofin and Germany's Deutsche Welle. Broadcasts from these blacklisted outlets were halted and their websites blocked as the Burkinabé authorities published a statement which said: "The media campaign orchestrated around these accusations fully shows the unavowed intention to discredit our fighting forces." Reporters Without Borders have called the suspensions "grave and abusive decisions".

## The Index

# PEOPLE WATCH

**DAISY RUDDOCK** highlights the stories of human rights defenders under attack

### Jina Modares Gorji

IRAN

Jina Modares Gorji is a feminist podcaster and blogger from the Kurdish province of Sanandaj in Iran – who advocates for women's rights. In May she was sentenced to 21 years in prison as a result of her participation in peaceful human rights activities. She was arrested a number of times for her role in the Woman, Life, Freedom protests in 2022 and has since been charged with disturbing national security and participating in propaganda activities against the state due to her work.

### Viktoria Roshchyna

UKRAINE

Russia's Ministry of Defence confirmed in May that Ukrainian investigative journalist Viktoria Roshchyna had been detained following months of concern over her whereabouts. An experienced freelance reporter covering crime, war and human rights, Roshchyna was in Russian-occupied territory reporting on the war when she went missing in August 2023. She has written about the Ukraine war for Index. Little is known about her situation and her family have been unable to contact her.

### Obert Masaraure

ZIMBABWE

Human rights defender Obert Masaraure was convicted in May of "obstructing justice" due to a social media post. Masaraure took to X to demand the release of his colleague Robenson Chere, who worked alongside Masaraure for the Amalgamated Rural Teachers Union of Zimbabwe (ARTUZ). ARTUZ is a trade union campaigning for teachers' rights and has been targeted by security agents in the state because of their legitimate work defending human rights.

### Sophia Huang Xueqin

CHINA

Investigative journalist Huang Xueqin played a significant role in the MeToo movement in China. In 2017, she surveyed hundreds of female journalists about their experiences of sexual harassment, publishing her findings a year later. In 2019 and 2020 she was charged with "picking quarrels and provoking trouble" after writing about protests in Hong Kong. The following year she disappeared. She was sentenced to five years in jail in June for "inciting subversion of state power".

---

# Sole survivor

Iranian filmmaker **VAHID ZAREZADEH** says being forced from his homeland and experiencing a multitude of losses has left him in despair

I've written and erased this many times. What is inspiration? What kind of question is that? For someone like me, who has been exiled from my country for making a film, with all my possessions confiscated, facing five years in prison and two years of exile, what can possibly be inspiring?

Almost everyone who has inspired me over the years, who has given me energy and good feelings, is either imprisoned or no longer in this world. Reflecting on this, the state of being without a homeland and the multitude of losses can lead me to believe that inspiration and

hope never existed.

But please, don't be disheartened!
I am my own hope, my own inspiration. This isn't coming from

CREDIT: Hromadske (Roshchyna); Frontline Defenders (others)

## Ink spot

As Index went to press, we learned that Iranian activist, artist, and cartoonist Atena Farghadani had been sentenced to six years in prison: five years for "insulting the sacred" and one year for "propaganda against the State".

Farghadani had been detained since 13 April 2024 after attempting to display a drawing in a public space, not far from the presidential palace in Tehran. Over the past decade, she has been regularly monitored and harassed due to her art and activities opposing the repression of rights in Iran, especially those of women and children.

She was detained in 2014 to 2016 and again last summer, when she claims she was poisoned. She says she was violently beaten after her recent arrest.

This powerful cartoon, by Jean-Baptiste Zappetti aka Zap, is named after her.

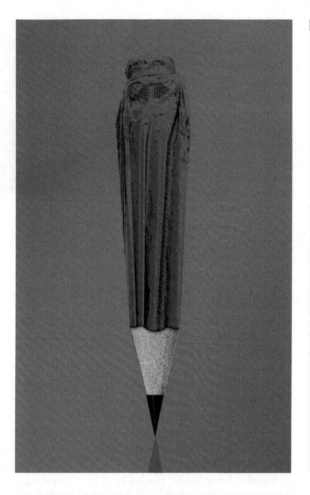

## Free speech in numbers

**122** The number of musicians, artists, writers and activists who signed Index's statement calling for Toomaj Salehi's death penalty to be quashed

**240** The number of seats won by Narendra Modi's BJP in the Indian elections, 130 fewer than expected

**4.2 billion** People who are facing a crisis of freedom of expression, according to a recent Article 19 report

**6** The number of pro-democracy activists from Hong Kong who had their passports cancelled in June

**20** The number of years faced in a Russian jail by Evan Gershkovich who has been formally charged with espionage

---

narcissism. I am the sole survivor of myself, and I now believe that I only have myself, and I'm trying harder than ever to learn to love myself. To embrace myself in loneliness and failure and to carry the heavy burden of my own existence.

Every morning, I place my phone far enough away that I have to get out of bed to fetch it. I drink ready-made coffee, take a cold shower. Under the shower, I sometimes laugh, cry, scream, or dance. I take my beloved Asentra pill for my depression and go to the city library.

I loved my books, I still do, but I no longer have them. In their absence, I dive into the library of the city I live in. I have managed to secure a regular table in the reading room that is often empty.

By paying one euro, I can temporarily own a small locker. There's an electronic membership card, but since I don't know German yet, I only use it for the toilet facilities. Now I've learned to write more, edit, sleep, and dream of films.

My latest film, about Narges Mohammadi, has started its editing phase. Narges, however, has to spend over twenty years in prison. In the absence of my cameras and computers, which were seized by security forces in Iran, I'm now making films with what I have and what I don't. A mobile phone, a cheap light, and a microphone. These are for when I need an artistic confrontation with the world outside myself. I've titled my films "Me and My Confrontations."

My confrontations with the world of migration, people, longings, beautiful and free women (something I didn't see in my country), food, dogs, laws and limitations, and the people in my dreams whom I don't have. All these presences and absences are the inspirations of my days. I just need to face them and myself in a more beautiful and better way. ✖

# The Index

TECH WATCH

# Sending a signal to the watchers

**MARK STIMPSON** says that the latest developments at Signal show why it must be sustained

IN THE SURREAL 1960s television series The Prisoner, lead actor Patrick McGoohan's cry for help in understanding the unusual environment he wakes up in has become legendary – "I am not a number, I am a free man".

You might wonder whether the bods behind Signal, the communication platform of choice for many dissidents, have taken note of his plaintive cry. The platform has been widely used by human rights activists at risk because of the platform's approach to privacy. Messages are end-to-end encrypted and everything from your name and profile photo to your contacts remain private.

Signal has now gone one step further. At the end of April, the platform announced it was changing the way that people are identified on the platform. Users will be allowed to keep the phone number they use to sign up a secret.

A phone number will still be needed but it can be hidden from other people. Previously if you were part of a protest organising committee and another contact had their phone compromised or seized, your phone number would be at

risk of discovery by bad actors.

No longer. Now phone numbers are no longer visible by default on the platform. Signal has also announced that users will be able to connect to others by choosing a unique username. These usernames can be changed at any time so if a group gets compromised a change of username makes you unfindable again.

Signal has changed the way people can be found on the platform too. You can make it so that only people who know the exact form of your username can find you.

It is an admirable upgrade for the people we care about most – dissidents. However, privacy tools do not come cheap.

Last December, Signal's president Meredith Whittaker and developer Joshua Lund published a blog post explaining how much it costs to run the platform – an estimated $50 million a year by 2025 they estimate. A big chunk of this comes from registration fees for sending verification codes to user's phones while millions more is spent on servers, despite only using them for temporary storage of messages before they are deleted.

Signal is a non-profit, funded by donations, small and large and they desperately need more of them. "As a nonprofit we don't have investors or profit-minded board members knocking during hard times, urging us to 'sacrifice a little privacy' in the name of hitting growth and monetary targets," they wrote.

They are clear that other tech platforms pay for the free services they offer consumers in troubling ways. Many tech companies offset costs by selling your data indirectly (or directly) to advertisers or by using it to train AI models.

"The cost of most consumer technology is underwritten by surveillance, which has allowed people to assume that 'free' is the default, and a

ABOVE: Patrick McGoohan in the surreal series The Prisoner. "I am not a number, I am a free man"

handful of industry players have accrued eye-watering amounts of personal data and the unprecedented power to use that data in ways that are shaping our lives and institutions globally," the pair wrote.

"To put it another way, the social costs of normalised privacy invasion are staggeringly high, and maintaining and caring for alternative technology has never been more important."

Back in the world of The Prisoner, in the final - and highly confusing - episode Patrick McGoohan is judged by a jury including anarchists and activists.

The jury is told: "He has revolted, resisted, fought, held fast, maintained, destroyed resistance, overcome coercion. The right to be a person, someone or individual. We applaud his private war, and concede that despite materialistic efforts, he has survived intact and secure."

McGoohan is finally told he has the right to be an individual and is allowed to meet his oppressor. It turns out to be him. Many things are left unexplained and this has led to wild fan theories about what it all means.

Let's hope Signal allows that to happen in the real world. So, to end I ask you on behalf of all the dissidents for whom Signal is a lifesaver – quite literally – do what I did and donate. ✖

CREDIT: ITC

# FEATURES

"It seems that when it comes down to it, if a parent complains, the book's gone"

# Banned: school librarians shushed over LGBT+ books

A special investigation by Index's **KATIE DANCEY-DOWNS** reveals more than half of UK school librarians surveyed by Index have been asked to remove books from their shelves

N A SECONDARY academy in England, a librarian is putting books into a box. Just moments before, they were proudly on the shelves, rainbow flags waving across their covers and words such as "queer" and "trans" shouting from their titles.

Now they are being sealed beneath cardboard and packing tape, the flags furled and titles whispered.

Emma, not her real name, was asked to remove every book with LGBT+ themes from her school library in 2023. She was given little information about the sudden need to purge the library of this content. She knew only that one parent had made one complaint about one book.

The pupils asked her where the books had gone.

"I can scarcely believe that because one book was challenged, the whole collection was removed," she told Index.

The books were hidden from sight and, although most have now been returned to the shelves, a handful of them have permanently vanished.

Since the incident, Emma has felt nervous about buying particular books for the library, a huge departure from the initial excitement she had for creating an inclusive and diverse collection. She tentatively bought a copy of the most recent Heartstopper book – a British LGBT+ graphic novel series about young people coming of age – but has found excuse after excuse to avoid putting it in the library. She wanted to

buy The Fights That Make Us, but knew that the Pride flag emblazoned on the cover would be a step too far.

"I feel frightened, intimidated," she said.

For Emma, the only explanation for the books' removal is an underlying homophobic attitude in the school, which she says has a Christian ethos (although it is not a faith school). A single complaint led to sweeping censorship.

Emma's experience is just one of many that have come to light during our investigation into book censorship in British school libraries. It was prompted by a comment from author Juno Dawson – the third most censored young people's author in the USA – who told Index in 2023 (Index vol 52.3 p66) that she had no idea whether her books were censored in the UK.

Since our interview with Dawson, we have spoken to numerous school librarians, talked to bodies which support them, sent out surveys and filed Freedom of Information requests to try to answer two questions: Are people trying to ban books in UK school libraries? And if so, are they succeeding?

In an Index survey of UK school librarians, 53% of respondents said they had been asked to remove books, with more than half of those requests coming from parents.

Of those, 56% removed the book or books in question. Titles included This Book Is Gay, by Juno Dawson; Julián

ABOVE: Juno Dawson, author of This Book Is Gay

is a Mermaid, by Jessica Love; and the alphabet book ABC Pride, by Louie Stowell, Elly Barnes and Amy Phelps, as well as plenty of other titles featuring LGBT+ content.

Manga comic books were removed in some schools because of the perceived sexualisation of characters, other books following complaints about explicit or violent content.

Books challenged in several schools – but ultimately not removed – included

various Heartstopper books by Alice Oseman, which were accused of homophobic language, swearing and self-harm discussions. Young adult fiction also came under fire in many schools, with librarians usually able to hold firm in keeping their collections.

One was asked to remove a book for "racism against white people". They did not comply with the request.

Our overall sample was small. Only 53 school librarians took part in the survey which we distributed via the Chartered Institute of Library and Information Professionals (CILIP), the School Library Association (SLA) and on a school librarians Facebook page. But it is not the only evidence we collected. We heard plenty of anecdotal accounts from librarians and the organisations that represent them. A CILIP survey in 2023 found that a third of librarians in public libraries had also been asked to remove books. Even more worryingly there seems to be a lot of self-censorship - librarians not supplying books for fear of coming into conflict with parents and senior staff in religious schools or those thought to have a religiously conservative student body.

Alison Tarrant is chief executive of the SLA, which helps UK schools to develop their libraries. She said her ➜

# One parent had made one complaint about one book

ABOVE: Book banning has become more commonplace in the UK, often due to LGBT+ themes

→ organisation was aware of attempts to censor school libraries, and that the concern was on the minds of members.

"I doubt this is a new phenomenon. And it's probably been going on for as long as school libraries have existed," she said. "I wonder whether it's a symptom of the more polarised society that we're living in now, and that's why things have got stronger."

Recent conversations around book bans have been heavily focused on the USA, where the American Library Association's (ALA) latest report shows that requests for bans of unique titles increased 65% in 2023 from the previous year.

That's 4,240 different books being targeted.

There's a reason we know all this – the data is being collected.

In the UK, there is no equivalent to the ALA list. Stories of library censorship occasionally bubble up, but only when the story is interesting enough to hit the media.

Almost every school librarian who spoke to us wanted to remain anonymous, as they were concerned about losing their jobs if they spoke out. We've changed their names and left out other identifying details of their stories.

But there was one who was happy to put her name to her words, as she has done before. The first time Alice Leggatt spoke out on censorship, she wasn't given a great deal of choice, as the story surrounding the school she was then at hit the media.

## Outside influence

Leggatt had been working at The John Fisher School, a Catholic boys' school in Purley, London, for around nine months. She loved the school, and felt it was going to great lengths to be inclusive, although she now reflects that more traditional members of staff and the archdiocese were less progressive.

When she booked children's author Simon James Green to give a talk in March 2022, she never imagined it would cause a problem. She sent a letter home to parents about how they could buy Green's books ahead of the visit if they wished to do so, also noting that the event would continue on from LGBT+ History Month celebrations and mark World Book Day.

"Somehow, that letter made its way to a blog that was posted in Scotland – quite a far-right Catholic blog," Leggatt told Index.

That blog was Catholic Truth Scotland, which is now accessible only through web archives. It published Leggatt's letter, along with a call for the event to be cancelled and details of who to contact.

The anonymous blog editor described Leggatt's letter as shameful and the event as scandalous, writing: "Cancel culture is all the rage now, so let's not waste time in following this 'fashion'; this is a very serious matter and I've already heard the opinion expressed by one parent that for any Catholic school to organise such a blatant promotion of the LGBT+ 'lifestyle' is tantamount to child abuse."

The school chaplain sent letters to parents encouraging them to boycott. According to Leggatt, some parents withdrew their children from the talk, although others sent supportive messages.

"And then it came out that the diocese that week had instructed the school to cancel," Leggatt said. The school refused.

The governing body held an emergency meeting on the Saturday preceding the Monday event, where they voted to continue with the visit. And then the situation stepped up a gear.

"On Sunday evening, I got the call from my manager to say that the diocese had fired the entire governing body," Leggatt said. The visit was cancelled.

"I think it was a shock to many of us that the diocese used that power and did in fact have that power."

A joint statement came out from the SLA and CILIP, and school staff went on strike. But the visit did not go ahead.

Schools watchdog Ofsted visited the school for a snap inspection and its report criticised the archdiocese's attempts to remove the school governors and praised the headteacher for his handling of the events.

In an article on pages 22-23, Green describes how the debacle impacted him as an author.

"I know from other librarians who work in faith schools that the behaviour of that archdiocese was considered to be unusual. Generally, there's a kind of softly, softly approach

to these kinds of things," said Leggatt, who left the school. And with other books in the library dealing with much more challenging topics – such as teen pregnancy and drugs – the only issue around Green's books, as far as she saw it, was gay relationships.

"What I've since found really interesting, looking at the progression of what happened, is how closely it mirrors what is happening in the USA," she said. "It was the same arguments, the same shifting goalposts, and the fact that the initial complaint came from a group completely unconnected to the school."

As one of the only named censored school librarians in the public sphere, other librarians have contacted Leggatt about their own brushes with censorship. She says around 20 people have told her their experiences, and all the issues have stemmed from books about sex and gender. Something that often connects these stories, she says, is that everything is quickly hushed up. Experienced librarians are telling her that this is a new phenomenon, unlike anything they've seen before.

And she is also concerned about self-censorship because librarians are nervous. Some 89% of respondents said they were at least a little worried about the potential for censorship in our survey with 30% saying they worried a lot.

## A series of minor acts

Green's very public cancellation is not the only censorship that has happened in school libraries. One librarian told Index that in a private school with a Christian ethos, a senior member of staff removed all Philip Pullman books without explanation. When pupils asked her where they could find His Dark Materials, she trotted out the line that the school didn't have them.

"It made you feel disempowered," she said, adding that she felt that the knowledge and experience she held as a librarian was disregarded. "At the time I needed that job and wasn't in a position

# Because one book was challenged, the whole collection was removed

to ruffle any feathers."

Louise, who works in a library service providing books to a range of schools, was asked by one to swap books with LGBT+ representation for different titles. Although she didn't want to, she was left with no choice but to comply.

She described how she worked in a predominantly Muslim area, where senior staff were not from the same background, and took pro-active steps to avoid confrontation.

"We've all seen what happened in Birmingham," she said, referring to the months-long protests outside a primary school in 2019 against the teaching of LGBT+ relationships. "No one wants to be like that school."

At some schools, she doesn't bother offering particular books in the first place. "If I'm buying for a school, I have to consider carefully how much the headteacher will back me," she said.

"Over here in the UK, it's soft censorship. It's easy in the USA – they have this handy list."

Amy lost a job over her refusal to censor a book which was perceived to be about LGBT+ issues. At first, the headteacher told her a couple of parents had complained about the book, and then came a written complaint from a conservative Muslim family. Amy argued that talking about equality was part of her remit as a librarian, and that the school should not assume the rest of the Muslim community would have the same reaction.

She was blamed for the upset, and for making the book available. She was asked to leave.

"What I draw the line at is when →

→ that school says that no child can see that book because one parent has written a complaint," she said.

She was supported by senior members of staff and others, but she lost her position regardless.

In another school, a parent suggested that a specific book be restricted to older children, and Amy was happy to oblige. But the decision was made that the book should be removed completely.

"It seems that when it comes down to it, if a parent complains, the book's gone," she said.

Another anonymous school library service worker, who we'll refer to as David, said that his organisation received complaints about LGBT+ content from all faiths, and explained that while headteachers were generally supportive, they haven't got the tools to formulate a defence.

He told Index that policies from groups such as CILIP and the SLA made no impact without a supportive school, describing a landscape where headteachers wanted to take the path of least resistance to shut down complaints. That usually means censorship.

"It's a very small minority of parents, sometimes just one or two, who want to kick up a fuss because they basically say for whatever reason, whether it's personal, social or religious, 'I don't want my child accessing this content'.

"And it's trying to get that message out saying, 'OK, you don't want your child accessing this content, but you can't shut it down for everyone else,'" he said.

## The books were hidden from sight and a handful of them have permanently vanished

"I think people are worried about upsetting certain groups," he said, explaining how there are some Muslim and Christian parents in his area who don't want their children exposed to LGBT+ characters. But, he stressed, these groups are not homogenous.

"We haven't even got a central government that's going to address this," David said, speaking in April 2024 before the election was called. "What we've got is a political climate where they're stoking these fires."

He described a librarian he knows in a private school who is handing out "off-the-record loans" from a back cupboard.

"There's nothing inappropriate. It's just stuff that they know the parents will disagree with," he said. In another private school, a parent tried to get a librarian sacked because their child had been reading an LGBT+ book.

In some cases, the censorship is more subtle. The SLA told Index that it has had reports of senior staff having a quiet word with librarians, telling them to keep particular books on the shelves but not to include them in displays.

"It also very much puts that librarian in a difficult position, because the children who need those books are only ever going to get them if they're directly signposted to them," the SLA's Tarrant said.

Gwen works in a school library service, supporting around 420 schools. She said that most of the book challenges the service faced were from secondary schools, and were usually based on the label given to a book or its content.

On one occasion, when it was running a book award for Year 8 pupils (12 to 13-year-olds), it was challenged on the inclusion of some books, including one with a minor LGBT+ element. One secondary Catholic school decided not to give that book to its students.

That same school refused to have a book which promoted open conversation around menstruation.

"Probably more of the challenges may come in from our Catholic secondaries," Gwen told Index. "And

ABOVE: Parents protest outside a school in Birmingham over children being taught about LGBT+ identities

we still have some Catholic primaries who don't have Harry Potter and books like that on their shelves."

But, she explained, the service has a robust policy, and encourages schools to do the same. It also runs seminars on how to tackle censorship attempts.

"I think it's just slight challenges," she said. "I think parents are challenging schools more and more about lots of different things. So, it isn't just censorship."

Gwen isn't as worried about censorship as some of the other library professionals we spoke to.

"I think it's just so that we're not leaving some poor, single-staffed library person to deal with any challenges that come in, that we give them all the tools to be robust in any answers," she said.

As well as surveying librarians, Index sent out FOI requests to a selection of schools. One Catholic school in Coventry confirmed that its headteacher complained to the local school library service about a handful of books which contained "inappropriate language and didn't support the Catholic ethos of the school".

The four titles contained themes of crime and the supernatural. They were replaced with different books.

Another – a comprehensive boys' school in London – told Index that

a pupil had requested the removal of Salman Rushdie's books, but that his request was refused.

The school library service in Milton Keynes works with primary schools. In response to an FOI request, it told Index that it had never had a book rejected by a school but had received negative feedback about a children's picture book of Chaucer's Canterbury Tales by Marcia Williams, owing to an abundance of "naked bottoms" and other bawdy content. It added: "It is also worth noting that it tends to be the faith schools that do have higher standards, or are more censorious," later adding that it avoided sending books about witches and wizards or with anti-faith themes to Catholic schools.

Several schools and school library services claimed they had not had book-challenge experiences. Many others failed to respond to the FOI requests.

Ofsted said it had found no evidence in inspection reports of censorship in school libraries since April 2021, although it also acknowledged that the automated search method meant this was not a guaranteed result.

A spokesman said: "It is for schools to decide what they include in their own curriculum, within the requirements of the law and the Department for Education (DfE)." He added that a good curriculum must ensure "that pupils understand, appreciate and respect difference in the world and its people, as well as engage with views, beliefs and →

## Some parents withdrew their children from the talk, although others sent supportive messages

→ opinions that are different from their own in considered ways".

Nick Cavender, the chair of CILIP's School Libraries Group (SLG), told Index that school librarians had always been aware of censorship.

"I don't think we are at a stage where we can see any particular patterns," he said. "But as professional librarians we need to bear in mind our duties to promote intellectual freedom and oppose censorship, while at the same time making sure that our collections meet the needs of our users – the school community."

### Top-down attitude
Like Leggatt, David said that every complaint he had heard, bar one, had stemmed from books with LGBT+ themes, and that it had escalated in the last couple of years. He said that the government's attempt to ban gender identity discussions from sex education has had an impact on his conversations with schools.

"Some schools, for example, have said, 'Well, we can't have books that discuss LGBT characters, because that links to sex education, and therefore we can't have that in primary schools'," he explained.

While the USA has an organised system of book challenging, spearheaded by chapters of right-wing Christian groups and politicians, the librarians who spoke to Index haven't seen anything particularly organised in the UK – although David does have

concerns about the influence of agitator groups who protest drag queen story time in libraries, and he said they "seem to be getting their scripts from the American playbook".

On online forums, book-banning sentiment is inseparable from the culture wars around sex and gender. In one Mumsnet thread, a user seeks guidance in drafting a complaint about the book She's My Dad due to the links with gender identity, later adding: "I'm really looking for experiences and complaints about this book/author, and how to write to ask for it to be removed/ immediately stopped being used until a parent consultation has gone ahead."

There are dozens of replies. Some offer advice, others cry "inappropriate content", and others argue that teaching the book is a political move.

The Safe Schools Alliance UK (SSA), a group which describes itself as "a grassroots organisation which campaigns to uphold child safeguarding in schools", ran a review of Juno Dawson's young adult novel Wonderland, beginning: "We had our ex-English teacher reviewer read it so that you – and your kids – do not have to."

The review was less than favourable. Out-of-context scenes are plucked from the book, peppered with dismissal of protagonist Alice's gender identity and accusations of "male sex fantasy tropes" and the "reckless statements Dawson plants in Alice's mouth".

Another group, Transgender Trend, which uses the strapline "No child is born in the wrong body", has published a lengthy essay on "trans picture books for little children" and describes some of them as "militantly activist".

A number of school librarians also told Index about FOI requests their schools had received.

They ask about LGBT+ material in their schools and whether those books are being used to "encourage the acceptance" of transgender identities. The feeling from librarians is that the FOIs are sent to be an agitation.

### A censorship-free future?
Having worked in school libraries for a long time, David believes a recent uptick in complaints is related to the wealth of available LGBT+ material that wasn't around before – a sentiment echoed by others.

He wants to see a top-down approach, a central message so that headteachers know they will be protected. Others want to see professional bodies taking the problem more seriously and libraries becoming statutory.

Many of the librarians who spoke to Index reported feeling on their own. Tarrant said the SLA had training and an advice line, but would also be reflecting, following Index's investigation, to consider how it can increase support.

"I would urge anyone going through a situation to pick up the phone and call us or to reach out on socials," she said.

Cavender said that CILIP members could also seek support from the SLG, adding: "It can be difficult as a school librarian as we work within schools and we have to be mindful of the culture and demographic of the school community. However, we still have obligations, such as under the Equalities Act 2010, to provide information for all our borrowers."

There are mixed feelings from librarians on whether an ALA-style list of challenged books would help or hinder the UK's fight against censorship.

Is it a way to shine a light on a growing problem or a ready-made list of targets for those who want to purge school libraries of particular material? For the SLA, a small national charity with six members of staff, the first problem with this approach would be the resources needed.

"I also think you'd have to have very careful consideration of what happened with that list afterwards," Tarrant said. "I hesitate about inflaming the situation."

She also worries about the wellbeing of authors who might find themselves on that list.

ABOVE: School libraries in the UK are a new battleground for censorship

"It's not to say that having one wouldn't necessarily be helpful in terms of having some sort of data on how much it was going on," she said. "But I'm not sure it's a solution in and of itself."

CILIP and the SLG's position is to monitor the situation.Cavender said that having "a robust collection development plan can guide school librarians and it can help get school management on board".

Tarrant said that the DfE position is for headteachers to make the best decisions for their schools, adding that as every school was different, there did need to be the ability to respond to local contexts. But that doesn't help headteachers looking for advice.

In the meantime, many librarians are proactively fighting for the freedom to read. Some, Gwen explained, are looking at the lists of banned books coming out of the USA and actively choosing them for their libraries. David's school library service puts together recommended reading, with a good cross-section of representation.

"We know that children are more likely to read if they're reading about stories, and characters and situations, be they fact or fiction, which relate to them," Tarrant said. "It is about allowing all children to understand the world that they're operating in, through imagination, through facts and through stories."

School libraries shouldn't be a battleground for cancel culture and librarians can't be expected to deal with censorship by themselves. With a new UK government, it is an opportunity for Ofsted and those who represent teachers and librarians to demand an end to this pernicious practice. ✖

*Katie Dancey-Downs is assistant editor at Index*

53(02):14/21|DOI:10.1177/03064220241270325

BOOK BANS

# We're not banned, but…

The cancellation of an author visit in 2022 set the stage for how UK schools would deal with books containing LGBT+ themes. **SIMON JAMES GREEN** reflects on his experience

O UT OF ALL the things on my author "bingo card", being on the receiving end of so much hate and feeling so threatened weren't among them.

Within days of having my visit to a secondary school in south London cancelled by the Catholic Archdiocese of Southwark, I was being told – via burner email accounts, anonymous social media posts and online blogs – that I "deserved to die and burn in hell", that speaking in a school about my LGBT+ young adult novels was "tantamount to child abuse", and that "a homosexual author of teenage fiction visiting a Catholic school is 100% as much of an issue as the war in Ukraine".

Part of me wanted to laugh at the hyperbole. But another part was genuinely terrified. My publishers had to ask other schools I was booked to appear at not to publicise the events – the abuse may have come from keyboard warriors but, when people are that extreme, caution is sensible.

The justification for the ban was hard to pin down, and it wasn't until months later that the governors of the school informed me the decision was based on a particular passage of my debut novel which they deemed offensive to Christians.

Taking the passage out of context (which of course they did, because book banners always do), some might think they had a point. But their argument was based on a complete misinterpretation of a scene which illustrates how anti-LGBT+ hate can permeate all areas of a person's life (including, in this instance, a prayer in assembly), and, ironically, how

≡ Part of me wanted to laugh at the hyperbole.
≡ But another part was genuinely terrified

CREDIT: (headshot) YellowBelly; (others) Simon James Green

some people weaponise religion for homophobic purposes.

It wasn't all doom and gloom, though. The support from the publishing industry was robust, while school librarians stood shoulder-to-shoulder with me – many of them booking me for a school visit "to make a point".

Students at several schools around the country made banners and leaflets to protest against the ban and to show support for their peers who wouldn't now get to benefit from my event. Meanwhile, I ploughed all my frustration into my semi-autobiographical novel Boy Like Me, about growing up under Section 28 (a UK law banning the "promotion of homosexuality" by local authorities).

My experience back then had many parallels with this one, and the book ultimately got me longlisted for the Yoto Carnegie Medal.

# As a writer it makes me second guess myself. Should I include an LGBT+ relationship in my next novel?

Heartening stuff. But fast forward two years and it feels to me like we're in an even more precarious position. The publicity the banning brought means librarians often want to talk to me about censorship issues, and many of them have been receiving more pushback about LGBT+ library books than ever before (see investigation on pp14-21).

As a writer, it makes me second-guess myself. Should I include an LGBT+ relationship in the next novel? Do I include details that gay kids will find authentic, or helpful, or will the book not sell to schools if I do?

It's worrying. I worry about the

impact falling sales of LGBT+ titles might have on publishers who then decide they're not profitable enough. I worry about the authors who can no longer tell their stories.

But I mostly worry about the young people in schools who so desperately need these books and need to know, whatever they're going through, they're not alone. ✖

*Simon James Green is an award-winning author who writes for children and young adults*

53(02):22/23|DOI:10.1177/03064220241270326

PICTURED: Simon James Green made headlines when he had a school talk cancelled

# The red pill problem

A misogynistic corner of the internet is silencing Muslim women, both online and in real life. **ANMOL IRFAN** meets the victims

WHEN THE FATHER of Ilsa's children died in 2019, she felt a worrying shift in her eldest son.

The 46-year-old single mother – a Muslim convert from eastern Europe – had been raising her three children on her own in London.

But now, in his early 20s, her son had become heavily invested in online communities led by Muslim men, and would spend all day on his laptop.

These communities, she soon realised as he became more vocal about his opinions, were what many people online know as "Muslim red pill", or "Muslim incels" or "Mincels".

Incel is a term used to describe men who are involuntarily celibate and are hostile towards those (often women) who are sexually active. In some parts of the men's rights movement, the term "red pill" describes the belief that women have all the power and men are oppressed.

One example of the type of content Ilsa's son saw as a result of following these personalities – or, in the Muslim context, "*akh* right bros" – is a video put out by influencer Sneako that went viral after he argued that women could come to God and to Islam only through a man.

Javad Hashmi, an Islamic studies scholar at Harvard University, explained to CNN that "*akh* right bros situate themselves in opposition to so-called Western values in favour of a version of Islam that is rife with misogyny".

A lot of these male influencers create content that is meant to be in direct opposition to feminism. They claim these views are the true essence of Islam.

While Ilsa (not her real name) tends to stay away from such conversations online, and explained that she never interacted with such influencers, she saw first-hand the very real offline harm these mindsets can cause.

"I am very aware of what my children are going through, as a single mother," she told Index.

"I was aware online conversations have an impact on him, but he never said such idiotic things until his father passed away – then he became more expressive that he agreed with people like [influencers] Daniel Haqiqatjou and Ali Dawah."

When she tried to have a conversation with him, her son would act as though Ilsa didn't know what she was talking about because she was a woman. He used examples he found online to tell his mother that she was good only for doing housework.

This was even though, as Ilsa pointed out, she was a single mother providing for him while he spent the whole day behind his computer.

"I had no support from him, financial or emotional, in terms of looking after his siblings or the house. He was more like a burden on me," she said, adding that last year he finally moved out – after she asked him to do so.

She had to make this difficult decision after he started displaying verbal aggression towards his sister, especially in matters of her clothing.

"As a mother it hurts, but I can't be crushed about it, because I believe even with bad there is good," said Ilsa. "Every relationship is different. Online you can just cut them off, but if it's someone in your family, Allah says you cannot cut off relationships

"However, you can put boundaries which are very, very needed."

While most people tend to see the

CREDIT: Associated Press / Alamy

Muslim "manosphere" – a general name for online communities promoting anti-feminism, misogyny and hateful ideas about women, trans and non-binary people – as being an online problem, fewer see its real-life implications.

Much of the popularity of this culture is linked to Muslim male influencers

ABOVE: Women's rights activists in Pakistan have taken to the streets to protest against gender-based violence

who preach Islamic content side-by-side with misogyny.

These "Dawah bros", as they've become known, often gain popularity through Instagram, X (formerly Twitter) and the podcasts they host.

"Existing Mincel culture is not an abnormality. It's actually an extension and acceleration of existing norms. That culture already existed – this just monetises it," said Dawud, a researcher on the manosphere who often calls out such behaviour online. He did not want to share his full name due to previous online attacks for speaking out.

He explained that the idea was inspired by right-wing populist influencer Andrew Tate's War Room, which charges nearly $8,000 for membership of what claims to be an "elite" men's club. →

ABOVE: Influencer Ali Dawah, who has been accused of spreading hateful rhetoric about women, clashes with British nationalist groups

→ Evidence gathered by the BBC suggests "generals" in Tate's War Room taught members how to groom women into sex work. Tate himself has denied wrong-doing and said he is prepared to defend his innocence.

Another way of making money, Dawud said, is by creating "rage bait" – content that will enrage viewers – which might include out-of-context clips used to incite criticism. When that content goes viral, the influencers earn money.

Many women in Pakistan who have interacted with such content online have told of men they knew who had never shared such beliefs but who had then gone down this path.

In one case, a male influencer messaged women he knew, telling them

he could no longer follow them because he was now religious. He asked them to keep following him so he could maintain his follower count on Instagram.

These tactics have formed a culture of "online Islam", where everything shared online needs to be approved by these so-called leaders, who often have little or no expertise in Islamic scholarship.

Instead, many of them are imitating a very white, right-wing conservative movement – which has historically been

Islamophobic – and combining that with their perception of Islamic beliefs to fight what they believe is the damage done by feminism to Muslim communities.

Yousra Samir Imran, a journalist and the author of Hijab and Red Lipstick, has regularly spoken out about the harms of red-pill culture, saying that even though

He used examples he found online to tell his mother that she was good only for doing housework

she used to engage with many of these men she has now stopped doing so because she feels it brings no benefit.

"When I saw people from the British Muslim community tweet something against women, I felt it was my place to stand up for my Muslim sisters," she said.

"However, then I would feel it would develop into a really unhelpful conversation online, and I felt like this is what they wanted and I'm adding fuel to their fire. It made them aggressive and made me stressed and anxious. So I just block or mute them."

Instead, she focuses on challenging beliefs through her newsletter and her writing, although she is aware that social media's echo chamber means her words won't always reach those who need to hear them most.

"Anyone can turn out this content based on their opinions, but they put this content out there as if it's researched. But it's not," Imran added.

Such content normalises a culture of hatred and ostracism, turning against anyone who fails to completely reject feminism.

"You need to bash Muslim women to maintain ideological purity," Dawud said of the Mincel culture, adding that even as a man he was not completely safe from their attacks. He has been called a fake Muslim, a *kafir*, a hypocrite and a conspiracist, but he says all this was tame compared with the way they treated women.

"They totally ignore and bypass facts like Prophet Mohammed (peace be upon him) helped with housework, and sewed his clothes," said Imran. "They just focus on the aspects of male companions being warriors or ultra-masculine, and use weak *ahadith* and out-of-context information to perpetuate their beliefs about women."

Sana (which is not her real name), an ethicist and medical student currently living in the USA, was one of the women who became victim to these attacks after she spoke out against Tate and the allegations of human trafficking. She had previously worked with victims of sexual

 It was when she spoke out against Tate that Pakistani men, who were his fans, found her account and decided to punish her for it

violence, including within legal settings, and often spoke out on this issue. But it was when she spoke out against Tate that Pakistani men, who were his fans, found her account and decided to punish her for it.It was only when they released photos of her much later – months after she'd deleted the Facebook account which contained them – that she realised they'd found the images much earlier and had been planning this for a long time.

"My response wasn't the best. I tried to deny it and ignore it and I should have immediately involved the police," the young medical student said, adding: "They found where I lived, started posting pics of my house, my number, found my workplaces and emailed them and even found all my friends. And the whole time I was trying to tune it out."

They didn't stop there. They leaked pictures of Sana's husband, calling him a rapist and making it seem like he was an ex-imam from Iran, which brought another wave of attacks on both of them. Then Haqiqatjou got involved. After Sana called him out, she says he attacked her online, and she consequently got him blocked from X for two months.

"The whole time this was going on I got so many death and rape threats. It affected my mental health and I had to step away."

She also pointed out that most of the accounts that doxxed her had additional accounts that focused on Islamic content. She couldn't comprehend how the two could ever go together.

In Pakistan, journalist Sajeer Shaikh shares similar beliefs. Shaikh, whose work often focuses on gender issues, said she used to moderate an online forum focused on feminism and saw similar content there as well.

"They would say things like, 'You are going against Allah's orders.' There were comments like, 'I hope a Taliban comes and beheads you and rapes your head,' and I was like, how do you put Allah and Taliban and rape in the same sentence?" she told Index.

Shaikh said she had learnt to tune these comments out, but added: "What has happened to our mentality? The increased aggression people have towards women is what bothers and upsets me because that has a definitive real-world impact and you see that in the wave of female murders in Pakistan. These things manifest in these ways when you allow them to exist in these spheres."

Sana now helps other women who have been victimised by men online to get in touch with police, file reports and use reporting mechanisms on social media platforms. She didn't have anyone to help her do that, and she said she went to the police much later than she should have.

"They did a Twitter space where they actually planned how to doxx me, and there was a girl in that space who was pretending to be a guy and she recorded it and sent it to me. I later sent it to the police. I should've sent that to the police at that moment because it showed intent."

When Sana sent the recording to the police, they told her it was exactly what they needed.

The weaponising of misinformation by Mincel groups is not only stirring up hatred but also leaving all who dare to speak out at real risk.They are silenced, they are losing family connections and they are at risk of physical harm. ✖

*Anmol Irfan is a freelance journalist based in Pakistan*

53(02):24/27|DOI:10.1177/03064220241270327

# Postcards from Putin's prison

A Russian teenager who tried to set fire to a military recruitment office to make his anti-war stance heard writes from his jail cell to **ALEXANDRA DOMENECH**

YEGOR BALAZEIKIN, A 16-year-old student at a reputable St Petersburg secondary school, woke up in custody on 1 March 2023. A year later, in a letter he sent to Index from prison, he said: "That was one of the hardest moments since [my] arrest."

The detention facility was overcrowded, and Balazeikin found himself in a cell with five men, despite the law requiring minors to be held separately from adults.

"Luckily, the men turned out to be decent people," said his mother, Tatiana Balazeikina, speaking to Index from the family home in Otradnoye.

"Nevertheless, for Yegor, his life as he knew it, his childhood, ended the day he was put into custody."

Balazeikin was arrested in Kirovsk after an unsuccessful attempt to set fire to a military recruitment office. He acknowledged that he was the one who had thrown bottles filled with diesel – which failed to ignite – at the building.

"[The police asked him] 'Why did you do it?' [and he replied] 'Because I'm against the war'," Balazeikina told Index.

This was a year into Russia's full-scale invasion of Ukraine.

When Balazeikin's parents arrived at the police station on the night he was arrested, a group of officers, including FSB agents, were interrogating him. His rights had not been explained to him, including his right not to incriminate himself. He confessed that he had tried but failed to set another army recruitment office on fire a few weeks earlier, but nobody had paid any attention to that particular action.

"In the interrogation report, [Yegor] describes how much pain [the war] caused him and how unacceptable it is," Balazeikina said. "He speaks of a Ukrainian boy, a refugee from Mykolaiv [a city which was bombed by the Russian army]."

She said he had told the officers that his uncle, who joined the Russian army as a volunteer, died in the war – and that he was deeply affected by his death.

Asked whether he was "trying to affect the decision-making of the

LEFT AND RIGHT: Photos shared by Balazeikin's family, before and after his arrest

authorities with his actions", Balazeikin had replied that it wasn't his primary goal, and that, "above all, he wanted to resolve his inner conflict", his mother explained. According to her, he felt the need to set himself free from a sense of complicity with the government.

Balazeikin was initially charged with property damage, but after interrogation he was accused of attempted terrorism. Eight months later he was sentenced to six years in prison.

"Yegor was prosecuted not for his actions but for expressing his opinion," his father, Daniel Balazeikin, said. He highlighted that his grandfather was also punished "for having a point of view" – he was jailed for eight years under Stalin over a joke about the food at the kindergarten.

Later, Yegor explained to his parents why he didn't choose a peaceful method of resistance.

"The time of posters was gone," he said. For him, the military recruitment office was "the ultimate symbol of war". He insisted, however, that he was certain that there was nobody inside the buildings when he threw the bottles.

According to Russian human rights group Memorial, in a situation where thousands of peaceful anti-war protests had been suppressed, "[Balazeikin] didn't find any other way to express his opposition" – and his gesture was an attempt to draw attention to what he called "the madness of war".

Memorial listed Balazeikin as a "political prisoner" – although the group said it didn't always approve of

## I suddenly realised he's not a child anymore – he's a man, with a frown on his face

the actions of people recognised as such.

While on trial, Balazeikin was held in detention, where conditions are significantly tougher than those in a penal colony and which is why minors are typically placed under house arrest. He remained there for many months despite having autoimmune hepatitis, which rapidly deteriorated due to the lack of proper treatment.

"The early days were the hardest," Balazeikin wrote in his letter to Index. "But in the end, [every hardship] proved to be temporary."

He added that he suffered from a "lack of good, bright, kind people", and recalled that he found it especially tough "when a friend moved to another jail cell about a year ago".

His father added that most of the minors who were held with Yegor were charged with rape. For a time during his pre-trial detention, Balazeikin was denied access to books – "which he cannot live without," his mother said – including textbooks he needs to continue his education.

 # Yegor was prosecuted not for his actions but for expressing his opinion

The prison authorities did not give him the letters which were sent to him, either. His access to books and letters was eventually restored after pressure on the prison.

"I find joy in small things. That's the only way [to cope with the situation]," Balazeikin wrote. "For example, today I'll see my parents – there are so many things to discuss and to share."

Daniel recalled seeing his son through a glass window in the detention centre, saying: "I suddenly realised he's not a child anymore – he's a man, with a frown on his face."

In his letter to Index, Yegor reacted to the sudden death of opposition leader Alexei Navalny in an Arctic penal colony in February – news which hit political prisoners and their families the hardest.

"Some people live in fear their entire lives – Alexei wasn't one of them," he wrote. "He wasn't afraid, to live or to die, I'm sure of it." Balazeikin was judged by a military tribunal instead of a civilian court last November – "a tactic used by the authorities to put additional psychological pressure on him," his mother said.

Yet, despite intimidation, in his last word to the court he channelled the great Russian author Leo Tolstoy, saying: "The only argument in favour of continuing a war is that it has already been begun." He added: "When you are alone, ask yourselves: 'Do [we] still need this war?'" ✖

*Alexandra Domenech is a Moscow-born, Paris-based journalist specialising in women's rights in Russia*

53(02):28/29|DOI:10.1177/03064220241270328

# The science of persecution

A celebrated scientist is still being silenced because of his faith even years after his death. **ZOFEEN T EBRAHIM** talks to those impacted at a university in Pakistan

THIS YEAR'S THREE-DAY Abdus Salam Science Festival was scheduled for the end of May at the Quaid-i-Azam University (QAU) in Pakistan.

But just 10 days before the event was due to be held, the vice-chancellor's office received a visit from members of the Majlis Tahaffuz Khatm-e-Nabuwwat (MTKN). The MTKN is a Muslim religious movement that seeks to protect the belief in the finality of Mohammed's prophethood.

Following the meeting, the event was postponed – much to the dismay of the organisers. The administration provided no written communication, but the MTKN's visit had clearly accomplished its purpose. It claimed that the festival was being organised to commemorate the "enemy of Pakistan and Islam" and that Muslims in the country were "extremely angry" about it. In a letter addressed to the vice-chancellor, widely circulated on social media, the MTKN warned that if the event took place under the scientist Abdus Salam's name, it would amount to "treachery".

The letter "requested" the event be "cancelled with immediate effect" or be held under another Muslim scientist's name. QAU, they said, should not be involved in promoting "the Qadiani network or a person" belonging to the

Ahmadiyya faith. ("Qadiani" is widely considered to be a derogatory term used for Ahmadis.)

Salam, a theoretical physicist who died in 1996, is revered among many in the international science community for his unification of the weak nuclear and electromagnetic forces. He is the only Pakistani scientist to be awarded the Nobel Prize, which he shared jointly in 1979 with two American scientists – Sheldon Glashow and Steven Weinberg.

He is, however, reviled by many in Pakistan for belonging to the Ahmadiyya community. Constitutionally declared non-Muslims in the country in 1974, they endure persecution for their faith.

"They asked me to either change the name of the festival or cancel it," said Niaz Ahmad Akhtar, the university's vice-chancellor, talking to Index from Islamabad.

"I did not make any promises but assured [the MTKN] the administration will look into their request."

He added he had not read the letter the group left with him.

"I won't take dictation from outsiders," he said. "The event will be held once the exams are over – it will be up to the organisers what name they want to use."

Muhammad Jamil Aslam, a professor in the physics department and the

ABOVE: Theoretical physicist Abdus Salam teaching at Imperial College London

festival's chief organiser, is sceptical.

"We have to separate religion from science," he said, adding that the purpose of the festival was "purely scientific" and that cancelling it did not make any sense for a university.

Renowned Pakistani nuclear physicist Pervez Hoodbhoy, an associate of the late Salam who was invited to be the festival's keynote speaker, was not surprised at the turn of the events.

"Pakistan is filled with religious hatred of every shape and form," he said. "Salam loved Pakistan and did a lot for it, but that love was returned with persecution."

Hoodbhoy recalled that in 1980, when

## Salam loved Pakistan and did a lot for it, but that love was returned with persecution

Salam sought to visit QAU's physics department (founded by his student), members of the Islami Jamiat-e-Talaba, an organisation that preaches Islam at modern institutions, had threatened that "they would break [Salam's] legs" if he ever came on campus.

"We had been preparing for the festival since the beginning of the year, and it had received approval from our department head as well as the vice-chancellor," said Syeda Ibtisam Naqvi, president of the Quaid-i-Azam Science Society that had organised the event. "What has religion got to do with this festival?"

The QAU students have vented their displeasure on various social media platforms. They have called Pakistan "a country that promotes hate and intolerance" and one that neither

practises "true Islam" nor values "scientific research".

Some are angry, asking why "fanatics are given so much power" and why "actual heroes" are never celebrated.

Pirzada, a physics student who goes by just one name, said the students could not come out and protest openly for fear of a violent backlash from religious extremists, giving the example of the mob lynching of Mashal Khan, a university student in Khyber Pakhtunkhwa province in 2017, who was accused of blasphemy.

More recently, in February this year, a teenage girl wearing a dress with Arabic calligraphy was hounded by a frenzied mob, who accused her of blasphemy after mistaking the printed words for verses from the Koran.

The state has remained a passive

onlooker during all of this.

In the 1960s then President General Muhammad Ayub Khan appointed Salam his scientific adviser, when he established several leading science institutions such as the Space and Upper Atmosphere Research Commission.

Last year, Imperial College London named its central library after him. He had, after all, headed the college's theoretical physics department.

It means that while he may be reviled by some in Pakistan, the wider world ensures he is honoured and not forgotten. ✖

*Zofeen T Ebrahim is a freelance journalist based in Karachi, Pakistan*

53(02):30/31|DOI:10.1177/03064220241270329

# Cinema against the state

**ZAHRA HANKIR** reports on how Lebanese artists and performers are using the arts in the fight to save their country's identity

EBANESE ARTISTS ARE using the promotion of their cultural identity as a form of resistance – opening old cinemas, offering free theatre performances and film screenings, organising workshops and staging cultural events.

While it might seem contrary to concentrate on the arts when your country is facing economic collapse, there are skirmishes on its borders and the political class is locked in stalemate, Kassem Istanbouli, the leader and founder of the Tiro Association for Arts (TAA), believes it is a "public duty".

"The main thing is that art is for everyone, meaning that theatre and cinema are for the people," Istanbouli, a former director and actor, told Index. "We want people to get used to theatre and cinema, and to know them well."

The NGO operates across cities, villages and towns all over Lebanon. The transformed cinema halls allow locals not only to enjoy film and theatre but also engage in workshops and community events that foster a sense of collective identity.

## Art is against oppression, against corruption

The events include music, arts and crafts, contemporary dance, photography lessons and *hakawati* (the ancient Arab tradition of storytelling).

Since 2014, under Istanbouli's guidance, the TAA has evolved from a cultural initiative into an essential resource for Lebanon's underserved communities.

"One of our key goals is to decentralise culture from Beirut, spreading it to places that are typically underserved… It's not easy to do this in Lebanon," he said.

### Culture amid war

In southern Lebanon, the ongoing war in Gaza has exacerbated the already dire economic and humanitarian situation, with daily exchanges of fire between Hezbollah and the Israeli military.

Many residents, especially those in farming communities, have suffered enormous losses amid the fighting, leading to a massive displacement as more than 90,000 families have been forced from their homes – many of them losing their sources of income.

In Tyre and Nabatieh, where scores of displaced people have recently relocated, the TAA has sparked a small but significant cultural revival and offered children a creative outlet.

In this context, Istanbouli believes "theatre and cinema are an act of endurance, an act of will, and a way to honour the people and their resilience".

"We do what we do for those who have lost their homes through no fault of their own, and for the children who've done no wrong," he said. "The war has destroyed their livelihoods. It is our obligation to do this very small thing to help them."

In Tyre, the revival is significant. Before being closed for 30 years, the city's cinemas were gathering places for leftists and artists such as the Palestinian poet Mahmoud Darwish and the Lebanese composer Marcel Khalife.

Movies were brought to the city by sea from Greece and Palestine, and they

RIGHT: Kassem Istanbouli, the leader and founder of the Tiro Association for Arts, believes theatre and cinema are acts of endurance

were screened to packed audiences who came not just for entertainment but for a sense of intellectual exchange.

By reopening these spaces to the public free of charge, the association is

CREDIT: AP Photo/Bilal Hussein via Alamy

both resurrecting this cultural heritage and creating new avenues for dialogue and free expression.

### 'Peace arts bus'

As part of its outreach, the TAA also operates a "peace arts bus" that serves displaced Lebanese people, as well as Syrian and Palestinian refugees. The initiative transports children from schools to theatres and enables them to take part in handicrafts and painting, fostering integration into the broader Lebanese community. The bus, decorated with images of Lebanese artists, sets off from Tyre and travels around villages in southern districts to perform free mobile shows and has brought joy and a semblance of normality to children whose lives have been disrupted by displacement and war, Istanbouli said.

The association works with people with disabilities and special needs and has screened films for the deaf and the blind. It offers a programme for women and girls promoting "social-economic empowerment and recovery".  →

→   "We really enjoy the theatre; it helps us forget the war," says Batoul, one woman who takes part.

## Expanding reach

Years before launching the TAA, 37-year-old Istanbouli, who studied theatre at the Lebanese University, founded the Istanbouli Theatre alongside colleagues and friends with the vision of bringing street theatre "directly to the people".

The project later evolved into the Tiro Association, named after the Spanish word for Tyre. Today, the TAA operates four cinemas across Lebanon in Tyre, Nabatieh, Tripoli and Beirut, with plans to renovate another.

Initially, the nonprofit was heavily reliant on membership, donations and the contributions of volunteers without any formal employees. As it gained recognition and won awards, it attracted a broader support base. Cultural institutions and donor organisations became partners including Unifil and Unesco.

Today, the group – which has more than 300 members – thrives with the help of volunteers, particularly the youth who believe in the project which, according to Istanbouli, wouldn't exist without them.

Istanbouli said that the association had not experienced censorship, despite it being an ongoing issue in Lebanon. To remain apolitical, it has avoided accepting donations from politicians.

"Being free and independent is something we have maintained since the beginning of our initiative," the TAA says in its brochure.

It has further broadened its scope

## Any city that's without a theatre or a cinema is a dead city

ABOVE: A beggar sits at the entrance of the abandoned Empire Cinema in Tripoli, Lebanon. It has since been restored by Kassem Istanbouli as a theatre

by co-operating with global cultural centres and associations from countries including Brazil, India and Spain. A recent initiative, the Sudanese Film Week, drew attention to the migrant worker community.

## Overcoming challenges

In some ways, it is setbacks which have spurred the TAA into action. Amid and after a 2019 uprising spurred by the economic crisis, its volunteers, undeterred by the lack of electricity, took their activities into public spaces.

"We performed plays where we were telling people to not accept the status quo, to not accept what we see today, to not accept inflation, to tell them we have a role to play," Istanbouli explained. "The theatre was inciting them to think, 'We shouldn't accept this'.

"We were saying art is against oppression, against corruption. It was cinema against the state.

"Theatre and cinema today play an even more important role in times of crisis – it's not only during good

times that they're important. Theatre and cinema seek to provoke, to raise awareness, to shift societal views, to bring people together, to reflect what we live today. If we're living in a crisis, they will reflect the crisis; if we live in a war, they will heal the wounds of people. No matter what we're enduring, we want to reflect these realities in cinema, in theatre and in music."

As an artist, Istanbouli says his greatest ambition has been realised through the TAA. He has been able to foster cultural continuity and to leverage the arts to engage and unify communities across his country, centring on his hometown of Tyre.

"We are walking our own path. It is a path that resembles us and that resembles the people," he said. "Any city that's without a theatre or a cinema is a dead city. A city that has theatre and cinema in it has people within it who want to live, and who have something profound to offer society." ✖

*Zahra Hankir is a Lebanese writer and journalist. Her latest book, Eyeliner: A Cultural History, was published by Penguin in 2023*

53(02):32/34|DOI:10.1177/03064220241270331

CREDIT: AP Photo/Bilal Hussein via Alamy

# First they came for the Greens

**ALESSIO PERRONE, DARREN LOUCAIDES** and **SAM EDWARDS** look at the violent attacks being carried out against Germany's Green Party as politicians standing on an eco-ticket in the European Parliament elections suffers big losses

CREDIT: Sina Schuldt / dpa picture alliance / Alamy

O N 14 FEBRUARY, as the upper echelons of Germany's Green Party prepared to descend on the south-western town of Biberach for their annual meeting, demonstrators blocked access to the town hall with tractors, paving stones, sandbags and manure.

Things took a more aggressive turn when three police officers were injured by protesters hurling objects. Police intervened with pepper spray and a protester smashed a window of federal minister of agriculture Cem Özdemir's car. The Green Party cancelled the meeting because of safety concerns.

In the state of Thüringen, 200 farmers and demonstrators attempted to block roads to stop a company visit by vice-chancellor Robert Habeck. They insulted the company's employees and threatened to hang journalists. A week later, an angry crowd followed and heckled party leader Ricarda Lang in Schorndorf, in the southern state of Baden-Württemberg, until police stepped in – then the crowd attacked the officers, injuring some of them.

These attacks were far from isolated

incidents. In 2021, the party was the most successful of its kind in Europe and the poster child of the continent's hopeful environmentalist movement, having joined a government coalition for the first time.

Today, it is coming under attack – verbally and violently – unlike any other party.

According to German parliament figures, 44% of the politically motivated attacks recorded in 2023 targeted Green Party representatives, three times as many as their coalition partners or the opposition.

Early this year, another angry mob prevented Habeck, once one of Germany's most popular politicians, from getting off a ferry in northern Germany. In September 2023, a man threw a rock at party leaders at a campaign event in Bavaria. And earlier that year, Lang found a gun cartridge in her letterbox.

Violence against MPs and politicians is on the rise across the EU, and in May

ABOVE: The Green Party office in Bremen is vandalised, adding to the list of recent political attacks in Germany

Slovakia's Prime Minister Robert Fico was shot in an assassination attempt. But in Germany, this violence disproportionately targets Green Party politicians.

Local party members and supporters have refused to join the electoral campaign out of fear, according to Carolin Renner, a local party speaker in Görlitz, a far-right stronghold where the Alternative für Deutschland (AfD) party won 32.5% of the vote in the 2021 election. →

## The Greens are coming under attack unlike any other party

→ It's hard to pin down when the mood began to swing against the Green Party. "I think this hate was always there," Renner told Index, adding that it might have been when AfD drifted to the far-right around 2015.

But things took a turn for the worse in 2020 and 2021 when Covid restrictions generated massive anti-lockdown movements in Germany. At the end of 2021, the Green Party formed a government coalition with the centre-left Social Democratic Party (SPD) and the liberal Free Democratic Party (FDP).

"That's when it really got out of hand," Renner said. "We had people calling to say they were coming into our office and going to kill us and our families." People slapped stickers on the doors, others spat on the windows and others glued the building's doors so members couldn't get in. "I was handling all the reporting to the police at the time, and I had to file at least one report per week," she said. "It was pretty bad."

Since the 2021 election, several political parties have tried to portray the Green Party as an urban elitist movement out of touch with the population. It is a favourite target of the far-right AfD, and its representatives have recently said it was "not surprising" that it was coming under attack.

But other parties have joined in attacking them, too. "It seems that the Greens were identified as the main political opponent by several, very different parties," said Hannah Schwander, a professor of political sociology and social policy at Humboldt University of Berlin.

Markus Söder, the leader of the centre-right Christian Social Union in Bavaria, said the Greens were "the number one party of prohibition", falsely claiming it planned to ban meat, firecrackers, car washing and balloons. And the far-left party leader Sahra Wagenknecht has branded the Greens "the most dangerous party in the Bundestag".

Even Olaf Scholz, the German chancellor from coalition partner the SPD, said it "remains a party that likes bans".

"When you have politicians or the media who take up these narratives, that creates an atmosphere in which it seems legitimate to attack politicians – verbally, at first," said Schwander. "But as we see now, that translates into action as well."

The politicians' rhetoric was accompanied by an onslaught of online campaigns. According to Raquel Miguel, a senior researcher with EU Disinfo Lab – an independent non-profit that gathers intelligence on disinformation campaigns in Europe – Green Party members were the most targeted by hoaxes during the

2021 election year. She said that they exaggerated the party's inexperience and proposals, falsely claiming the party planned to ban fireworks or family barbecues, for example.

"Online campaigns contributed to stirring up hatred against individuals but also to discrediting and undermining trust in politicians, dehumanising them and making them more susceptible to attacks," Miguel told Index. "And dehumanising contributes to accepting violence."

In conspiracy-minded far-right groups congregating on the social messaging platform Telegram, the party was depicted as an enemy trying to "take

ABOVE: A satirical float depicting Green Party politicians is paraded at the Rose Monday carnival in Cologne

away your way of life, your steak, the sugar from your coffee", said Lea Frühwirth, a senior researcher with the non-profit Centre for Monitoring, Analysis and Strategy. "What that does psychologically is [make it feel] like an invasion of your personal space."

The media have reported that the attacks on the Green Party's annual meeting in Biberach and the heckling of the party's leader in February originated from conspiratorial Telegram channels.

Violence against the party is on the

rise, just as green parties faced the worst losses in the 2024 European Parliament elections. The party's share in Germany appears to have plummeted since the last elections. However, researchers say that the population has not turned against climate issues. "The data shows that there hasn't really been a widespread backlash against green policies," said Jannik Jansen, a policy fellow focusing on social cohesion and just transition policies at the Jacques Delors Centre think-tank within Berlin's Hertie School, which focuses on governance. Jansen co-authored a recent study of attitudes to climate policy among 15,000 voters in France, Germany and Poland. "The political mainstream hasn't really shifted in this sense," he said.

But polarisation and extremism have risen. Schwander said some climate issues had become more politicised, and society in general has become more polarised – although in a peculiar way. "People don't seem to be more polarised on issues than they were before, but they dislike people who think differently more," she said.

Political violence has risen considerably. Police recorded 2,790 incidents of physical or verbal violence against elected politicians in 2023 – and the figure has nearly doubled in the last five years. Attacks resulting in physical injury also appear to be on the rise.

Twenty-two politicians have been attacked so far in 2024, compared with 27 for all of 2023, according to federal police.

The number of politically motivated crimes has also risen to record-high levels, driven by a rise in right-wing extremism. According to government figures, the country recorded 60,028 offences in 2023 – the highest level since records began in 2001.

But things appear to be going better in the far-right stronghold of Görlitz. "This year, we only had maybe two or three direct attacks," said Renner. She said the biggest incident happened during the farmers' protests that shook Europe in late 2023 and early 2024.

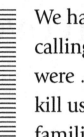

## We had people calling to say they were … going to kill us and our families

"Shortly before Christmas, someone dumped a big load of horse shit right in front of our door at the Zittau office," she said, adding that the decrease in attacks might be due to the police being more actively involved.

She said the party had also put in place a safety plan ahead of the European elections, requiring members to move in groups of at least three and sharing the list of party events and members' whereabouts with the police at all times.

Attacks seem to have spilled over to other parties. In early May, European MP Matthias Ecke, from the SPD, was seriously injured when four young men assaulted him while he put up campaign posters in Dresden. He had to be taken to hospital and required surgery. That same evening, a Green Party campaigner was assaulted in the same area, allegedly by the same group. And a few days later, it was the turn of AfD politician Mario Kumpf, who was attacked in a supermarket.

Renner told Index that someone tore down nearly every party's electoral posters in the northern part of the Görlitz district. "There's not one poster left except for the far-right," she said. "It's not just the Greens anymore – it's democracy itself that's being attacked." ✖

*Alessio Perrone, Darren Loucaides and Sam Edwards developed this article with the support of the Environmental Investigative Journalism grant programme of Journalismfund Europe*

53(02):35/37|DOI:10.1177/03064220241274926

# Undercover freedom fund

Writer **GABIJA STEPONENAITE** talks to the founders of Bysol, a non-profit humanitarian foundation using cryptocurrency to help dissidents in Belarus and aid the Ukrainian war effort

ANDREJ STRIZHAK, A human rights activist and Belarus exile, uses an electric scooter to go around the streets of Vilnius's old town.

"It is a very convenient means of transportation," he told Index, sitting in a coffee shop at The House of the Signatories where Lithuania's Act of Independence was signed in 1918.

Strizhak is founder of the Belarus Solidarity Foundation, Bysol, a humanitarian organisation which gives financial help to political prisoners, striking workers and other activists critical of the repressive regime of President Aliaksandr Lukashenka. Recently Bysol has also focused on aid to Ukraine in its fight against the Russian invasion that Vladimir Putin launched in February 2022.

For Strizhak, both struggles are connected.

"Belarus's 'freedom key' is in Ukraine, and many Belarusians are helping fight the war in Ukraine," he said. "If Putin fails, then Lukashenka will lose his principal ally."

His colleague, former male model, fitness trainer and media celebrity turned political activist Andrey Tkachov, joined us in the café. Tkachov like Strizhak is in his thirties. He's an immensely tall and striking figure, dressed in black. He oversees the management of the Medical Solidarity Fund, operating under the Bysol Foundation umbrella. He sees the conflict in stark terms.

"It is a war between good and evil.

Russia is knowingly bombing hospitals and we are working on getting medical supplies and equipment."

Bysol has raised over $10.7 million and acts as a platform for other organisations or individuals to raise funds for humanitarian causes.

Most of it has been done through cryptocurrency because, as Strizhak explained, it is "hard for the government to trace these transactions."

During the first days of the Ukrainian war, Bysol received requests for cash to buy vehicles, drones and first aid kits; funds were needed for emergency contraceptive and rape kits for Ukrainian war victims of sexual abuse and for legal fees to pursue justice for war crimes. Within a few days, Bysol raised over $130,000 for Ukrainian humanitarian causes and for Belarusian volunteers working in Ukraine.

As the war progressed, the foundation used its money to aid wounded Belarusian fighters to obtain medical assistance, move to Poland or Lithuania and heal from PTSD. Bysol handed over radios, sets of uniforms for medical doctors and anti-thermal camouflage cloaks to the Belarusians fighting in Ukraine.

They gave others help too.

For those who refused to fight or faced repression for opposing the war, Bysol staff drafted manuals on evacuation from Belarus, Russia and Ukraine. They also posted instructions in a Telegram chat group, BysolEvacuation. Users issued advice

on how to leave the war zone, discussed visa procedures and shared experiences on border crossings.

Strizhak and other activists first established Bysol in August 2020, as a response to violence against the opposition after the Belarus presidential election which saw Lukashenka winning a sixth term in office. Strizhak had already been detained several times by the police for his political activities and during the election summer, friends advised him to go on "vacation" abroad. He traveled to Kyiv, hoping to spend a month in Ukraine. There, building on his humanitarian work and crowdfunding skills, Strizhak came up with the idea of a fund-raising organisation.

He was joined in Ukraine by Tkachov, with whom he had worked during the Covid-19 pandemic and who had just been released from police custody. Tkachov had stayed in Belarus and joined anti-government protests in Minsk, witnessing police using grenades and shooting at peaceful opposition.

"The day after the elections, my friend and I took a ride around Minsk to check the aftermath of the protests," Tkachov told Index. "An OMON (special police force) car stopped us and took us to a detention centre." Officers gave Tkachov some "special attention" for his critical political opinions. He was handcuffed and beaten.

"Some of us fainted from the pain and from the inflicted injuries. We laid in puddles of blood and urine and prayed to be alive," he said. Eventually, he lost consciousness when a soldier stepped on his neck.

"I regained consciousness only when police brought me to the prison, and a soldier poured water on me," he said.

> ≡ If Putin fails, then Lukashenka will lose his principal ally

Together with the other 35 detainees, he spent three days in a cell suitable to accommodate 10 people.

In the late autumn of 2020 both dissidents decided to move to Lithuania, a member state of the EU and NATO, determined to expand Bysol. "Ukraine did not feel safe enough for us," explained Strizhak.

Strizhak first raised money through a friend in the Netherlands who opened a fundraising account on Facebook. "We couldn't do it from Belarus or Ukraine. Only people who live in 'the white-world' - the USA or Western Europe - can open fundraising accounts on Facebook," he said.

Medical doctors actively expressed their opposition to the government's actions. They were the ones who saw wounded, beaten, and dead protesters

Help started pouring in and more so when they were established in Vilnius. The most active supporters of the fund were and still are the Belarusian diaspora.

Walking a thin line between publicity and safety, Bysol has come to rely on cryptocurrency. Using traditional currency, customers rely

on bank services and often pay high fees for financial transactions that might take a few days to complete, but cryptocurrency is a digital  →

BELOW: Human rights activists Andrej Strizhak (right) and Andrey Tkachov have been forced to move to Vilnius in Lithuania to run the Belarus Solidarity Foundation, Bysol

→ currency based on a network spread across many computers, unregulated by central government authorities. Unlike traditional financial institutions, opening a cryptocurrency wallet does not require identification verification, credit, or background checks: a person needs just a laptop or a smartphone with an internet connection and there is virtually no way for the government officials to stop, censor or reverse these transactions.

People find Bysol through social media and by word of mouth and the foundation follows a rigorous verification process before providing any help.

"We can't name recipients and they can't say 'Thank you' to us," Strizak said.

Tkachov focuses on supporting

# I regained consciousness only when police brought me to the prison, and a soldier poured water on me

Belarusian medical professionals and medical causes.

"Medical doctors actively expressed their opposition to the government's actions. They were the ones who saw wounded, beaten and dead protesters. They described people arriving at the hospital as if they were brought from a battlefield with gunshot wounds or limbs ripped off by grenade explosions," he said. Many medical doctors who expressed their disagreement about the government's actions were laid off from state-run hospitals.

The Department of Investigation Committee in Minsk has initiated

criminal proceedings against Strizhak who is accused of providing "training of individuals to take part in group activities, grossly violating public order" and financing extremism. Bysol itself has been labelled an extremist organisation and Belarus has listed its founders on the country's wanted list and the wanted list of the Commonwealth of Independent States (CIS), made up of Russia and other ex-Soviet states still in Russia's orbit.

Tkachov said he was always interested in history, especially events leading to the outbreak of World War II. "I could not understand why the powerful states could not prevent it," he said. "Witnessing unfolding events in Ukraine, I finally understood it. When I think about how much more needs to be done, I worry my efforts are not enough, or are not effective enough. We need to help many people."

Since his early years, Strizhak was determined to bring change to society: "I can't tolerate hypocrisy, lies or double standards," he said. He travelled to the Donbas region of Ukraine from 2017 to 2020 to document war crimes committed by pro-Russian separatists. He has mourned the death of close work partners.

Although he is now far from the war zone, he visualises his efforts with a consciousness of the samurai way of "dying before going into battle." Like Japan's ancient warriors, he said, he is waging his humanitarian efforts fully committed and without fear. ✖

*Gabija Steponenaite is a writer and journalist for the website Ordinary Lives Extraordinary Stories*

BELOW: A protester labels Vladimir Putin and Aliaksandr Lukashenka "war criminals" during a gathering in London in solidarity with Ukraine

CREDIT: Vuk Valcic/Alamy

53(02):38/40|DOI:10.1177/03064220241271522

# A phantom act

**DANSON KAHYANA** reports on how Uganda's unconstitutional "mini-skirt law" still haunts the country

THERE IS SOMETHING curious about Uganda's Anti-Pornography Act (2014): it is a skeleton that breathes and walks in the sense that it still holds sway over the entire nation, despite its most important sections being declared null and void by the Constitutional Court in August 2021. Pejoratively referred to by civil society as the "mini-skirt law", the act defines pornography as "any representation through publication, exhibition, cinematography, indecent show, information technology or stimulated explicit sexual activities or any representation of the sexual parts of a person for primarily sexual excitement."

The emphasis on sexual activities and the sexual parts of a person shows the act's aim is to police sexuality and its representation, with attention to sartorial and artistic acts that are considered erotic or whose intention is perceived as erotic arousal. It is not surprising therefore that the act's victims so far are mostly women who were considered indecently dressed or too erotic for the public eye. Indeed, shortly after the act became law in 2014, two women – Jane Nabukenya and Prossy Nassuna – were detained for three hours each by Catherine Baguma, the Bukomansimbi District Grade One Magistrate, who found them in contempt of court for dressing indecently. In the same year, Jemimah Kansiime, also known as Panadol wa Basajja (men's painkiller), was charged under the act for promoting pornography in her song Nkulinze (Luganda for: I am Waiting for You). Its video shows her fondling her breasts as she dances erotically in anticipation of her lover whom she invites for a

shower. She denied the charges, but the producer of the song, March Didi Muchwa Mugisha, who was co-charged with her, pleaded guilty.

In July 2019, one of Uganda's top musicians, Winnie Nakanwagi alias Winnie Nwagi, was reported by Ugandan media to have apologised to the Pornography Control Committee for a show she had held at St Mary's College, Kisubi, a boys-only school in Entebbe, Uganda. Uganda Radio Network reported her apology as reading thus, in part: "I, Nakanwagi Winnie aka Winnie Nwagi of Swangz Avenue, do hereby acknowledge that my representation through indecent and erotic dancing during the music show held on 13 July 2019 at St. Mary's Kisubi was pornographic and contravened the provisions of the Anti-Pornography Act, 2014."

The act came into force in 2014, when Ugandan President, General Yoweri Kaguta Museveni, signed it into law. Shortly after, five organisations (led by the Centre for Domestic Violence Prevention) and four individuals petitioned the Uganda Constitutional Court to declare it null and void because several of its sections contravene the provisions of the 1995 Constitution of Uganda. Indeed, on 13 August 2021, the petition succeeded in part as the panel of judges, led by Justice Frederick Engonda-Ntende, declared five sections null and void for being inconsistent with the constitution.

The petitioners argued that the definition of pornography as provided in section two of the act was bound to lead to infringement on citizens' rights as it was too sweeping and imprecise. In the words of Justice Engola Ntende,

it "is too general and unacceptable as it may capture a range of conduct that is too wide and not intended to be subject to the offence". The court also found the powers granted to the Pornography Control Committee and the courts were unconstitutional. As Justice Ntende put it bluntly, "the activities of the Pornography Control Committee and the courts in relation to sections 12 and 15 of the Anti-Pornography Act equally [do] not pass constitutional muster."

Given that the entire act depended on the definition of pornography and the functions of the committee and of the courts of law, it goes without saying that what is left is just a shell. However, Charles Dalton Opwonya, who represents the Uganda Law Society on the committee, does not agree with this view. He argues that the judgement did not affect the committee's work. In fact, the day Index talked to him in May 2024, he was in the northern Uganda City of Gulu where he had been participating in the committee's work of sensitising the community about the Anti-Pornography Act. When Index asked him if the committee was not in contempt of the Constitutional Court that had declared its work unconstitutional, he argued that this was not the case as the court had not taken away the committee's power to teach the nation about the evil effects of pornography. When Index told him it appeared that the committee was concerned more with morality than legality, he argued that British common law, on which Uganda's penal code is based, is grounded in the Bible's Ten Commandments. →

The act's victims are mostly women considered too erotic for the public eye

LEFT: Ugandan musician turned politician Bobi Wine addresses a crowd in Hoima, Uganda

→  While defending public morality and decency are the main aims of the act, according to Oponya, there is fear that the act could be weaponised to stifle dissent as with the Computer Misuse Act (2011). At least two writers – Stella Nyanzi and Kakwenza Rukirabashaija – were arraigned in courts of law under this act (the Computer Misuse Act) for allegedly offending and cyber-harassing President Museveni. Nyanzi even got convicted for the latter offence although a higher court exonerated her after she had served more than a year of her sentence. Given the increasing role that artists are playing in Ugandan politics, there is the possibility that the government could use the act against the opposition - the leader of the biggest opposition party, the National Unity Platform, is Robert Ssentamu Kyagulanyi, also known as the singer and actor Bobi Wine.

It is significant that in Index's interview with Opwonya, he kept mistaking the Anti-Pornography Act with the Computer Misuse Act (2011) and the Anti-Homosexuality Act (2023). This underlines the fact that these acts are similar in intention – to unleash a legal regime meant to benefit the ruling party. To appreciate this point, we need to look at what happened in 2006, when President Museveni tried to use the courts to frustrate retired Colonel Kizza Besigye Kifefe's candidacy in the presidential elections by bringing a rape case against him. It turned out that Kifefe had never met the woman the prosecution alleged he had raped. In his ruling in this case, the presiding judge of the High Court, Justice John Bosco Katutsi, could not help but lambast the state for abusing the courts for political gain. In their article entitled Personalisation of Power Under the Museveni Regime in Uganda, Gerald Bareebe and Kristof Titeca cite part of Justice Katusi's judgment: "The evidence before this court is inadequate to even prove a debt, impotent to deprive of a civil right, ridiculous for convicting of the pettiest offence - scandalous if brought forward to support a charge of any grave character - monstrous if to ruin the honour of a man who offered himself as a candidate for the highest office of this country."

Further still, the fear that Museveni could weaponise the Anti-Pornography Act lies in the fact that its enforcement largely depends on the relevant minister, in this case the Minister of State for Ethics and Integrity, who is appointed by the President of the Republic of Uganda. It follows that the minister can use the act to go after people who are considered enemies (read: critics) of the sitting president, as has been the case with the Computer Misuse Act (2011).

Uganda finds itself in a tricky situation where advocates for freedom of speech, like Jemimah Kansiime's lawyer, Isaac Ssemakadde, believe that the Anti-Pornography Act is unworkable. The members of the Pornography Control Committee, on the other hand, believe that since the Constitutional Court did not declare the entire act null and void, they still have a role to play in fighting pornography. It is this unclear situation which is the ghostly existence of the act. True, Jemimah Kansiime is not in prison because the act under which she was charged is moribund, but she is not free either since the state prosecutors have not withdrawn her case. At any time, the skeleton that still walks and breathes called the Anti-Pornography Act could pull her into the cold cells of prison until her lawyer manages to get her out. ✖

*Danson Kahyana is a poet, author and scholar at Makerere University and Stellenbosch University, as well as Index's contributing editor for Uganda. Currently, he is a Fellow at the Carr Centre for Human Rights Policy, Harvard Kennedy School.*

53(02):41/43|DOI:10.1177/03064220241274928

# Don't say 'gay'

Identifying as LGBT+ could soon become an imprisonable offence in Ghana, and the uncertainty is creating a dangerous landscape, writes **UGONNA-ORA OWOH**

THE LGBT+ COMMUNITY in Ghana was gripped by fear on 28 February, when parliament passed a bill that would not only criminalise sexual practices but also punish anyone who identified as part of the LGBT+ community with three years in jail – or five years for anyone forming an LGBT+ group.

The bill was introduced in 2021 by Sam Nartey George and called The Proper Human Sexual Rights and Ghanaian Family Values Bill.

It led to outbursts from activists, scholars and Western corporations who were against it, but that only slowed its success.

The deputy director of LGBT+ Rights Ghana, Abdul-Wadud Mohammed, believes there's an underlying reason for the bill being resurrected and passed this year — a reason which has been overlooked by Ghana's media.

"I believe this year being an election year is a factor to consider," he told Index. "The bill was introduced by MPs of the opposition party. They are currently using it as a tool to gain political points going into the election in December."

The queer-bait election saga, where the government uses a minority group as a pawn to gain political favours from the public, is a common phenomenon.

And because queerness is seen as a huge taboo in most countries in Africa, LGBT+ individuals suffer.

A similar situation played out ahead of the 2015 Nigerian elections with the Same Sex Marriage Prohibition Act, and part of the driving force behind Uganda's Anti-Homosexuality Act could be to solidify President Yoweri Musevini's position before the next election.

With a battle line drawn, the queer community has been putting up a fight. In September 2023, Ghana witnessed one of the biggest demonstrations in a long time, the #occupyjulorbihouse protest – a play on the name of the president's office, Jubilee House, and the Ga words "*Julor Bi*", which means "child of a thief".

It was sparked by several things, including mismanagement of the economy and hardship but also the anti-LGBT+ bill which had just passed its second reading in parliament.

Queer Ghanaians joined the protest for erasure of the bill. Hashtags such as #killthebill and #WeAreAllGhana trended on X (formerly Twitter).

Justice Okai-Allotey, communications officer at the Humanist Association of Ghana, described the protest as peaceful – until the police raids.

"The police were against the protest. They were arresting people, trying to interrupt the protest," he said. "But after they saw people come the next day, because it was a three-day protest, they started backing down. Those arrested were later released."

When the bill was passed in February, queer Ghanaians were unable to protest due to the risk of getting assaulted or arrested. But they took to social media, staging campaigns against the bill and urging other queer Ghanaians and allies in the diaspora to protest. Protests took place in the UK, Germany and Canada.

One result of the bill is the heightened endangerment of queer lives in Ghana – both physically and in online spaces.

Owuraku Agyemang, an activist

 I'm keeping safe by mostly blending in, kind of inserting myself in the crowd, keeping a low profile and being less flamboyant

LEFT: Ghana's anti-LGBT+ bill has been met with large protests by human rights groups overseas, including this demonstration in London

criticising the bill and giving their opinions on it.

"[The] majority of people I know have an anonymous online presence, so that hasn't changed much, but people have been very careful of the places they visit to avoid violent homophobes," Okai-Allotey said.

Most public figures and celebrities have remained silent around the bill. And some Ghanaian blogs have openly supported it. "I think the media has already made its position clear on the bill," said feminist and activist Awo Dufie. "From the introduction of the bill, a lot of media houses have been specifically involved in targeted misinformation and disinformation, as well as platforming violence against the community."

With the unravelling chaos, people are having to adapt their lives in order to stay safe.

Kojo Marfo, a femme man, told Index: "It's a tough time but I'm keeping safe by mostly blending in, kind of inserting myself in the crowd, keeping a low profile and being less flamboyant. I just put up a masculine act in order to attract fewer eyes on me."

Although Ghana's president, Nana Akufo-Addo, has refused to give assent to the bill, a supreme court hearing is ongoing to debate the bill and its future.

Mohammed said: "I hope the supreme court's decisions on both of the cases filed against the bill will be of a progressive nature and help kill the bill so that the president wouldn't have to be forced to give assent to it." Despite the turbulent situation and the parallels with similar laws in Uganda (which did pass), the LGBT+ community in Ghana isn't losing hope. ✖

*Ugonna-Ora Owoh is a journalist based in Lagos, Nigeria*

53(02):44/45|DOI:10.1177/03064220241270333

and culture curator, has criticised the bill and aired their opinions alongside other activists and queer people. However, that has opened them to threats and cyberbullying from supporters of the bill. While it has bothered them, they've come up with a way to deal with the threats.

"I mostly deal with abusive content and cyberbullying with blocking," Agyemang told Index. "It's better for me to block and report them than to engage and interact with them to avoid the situation being mentally draining to me."

What Ghana's public may soon discover is the ease with which anyone can fall prey to mass jungle justice,

whether they are queer or not. It only takes a group of people to make an allegation against someone for them to become a victim. In August 2023, a video seeming to show a teacher beaten by a group of people flooded X. The teacher had been accused of being gay, based on hearsay. Accounts from commentators described the intervention of the police, who later made arrests, showing how the bill could damage Ghana's society if it ever passed into law.

Despite the risks, most queer Ghanaians aren't renouncing their identities, even on social media. The only thing close to it is their resolve to stay anonymous, but they are actively

# THREE UNHERALDED DISSIDENTS.
# THREE REMOTE ISLANDS.

# AN EXPLORATION OF WHAT IT MEANS TO HAVE AND TO LOSE A HOME.

'Fascinating.'
*OBSERVER*

'Breathtakingly good.'
EDMUND DE WAAL

'Brilliant.'
*THE ECONOMIST*

**OUT NOW IN PAPERBACK**

# SPECIAL REPORT

THE FINAL CUT

"BJP activists have succeeded in getting streaming
services such as Amazon Prime to apologise for
a show, Tandav, for denigrating Hindu deities"

WHEN THE ORIGINAL IS BETTER THAN THE REMAKE | SALIL TRIPATHI| P.65

SPECIAL REPORT ◆ THE FINAL CUT

ABOVE:
Controversial
films do get
made in the
USA but they're
unlikely to
attract big
distributors

# Money talks in Hollywood

**KAREN KRIZANOVICH** explores how profit is the deciding factor in stories left out of Hollywood

THE POWER TO decide who makes a Hollywood film has changed from the days of the cigar-chomping, overweight, overbearing white male mogul made famous in the Coen Brothers' movie Barton Fink. No longer does a single despotic studio head make the big decisions.

Instead, there are teams of people who not only have physical control over the enormous budgets needed to prep, produce and market a movie but who also have complex systems in place for its distribution, be that in cinemas, on streaming platforms or both. To find those people, simply follow the money.

How much does this say about the Hollywood narrative and the stories it leaves out, rather than the ones it tells?

Studios operate with an eye to their share price and those shareholders and stockholders expect big dividends. So, while we have the big Hollywood machine set up to produce whole worlds for us to watch, the magic of movies on a large scale still remains essentially a huge money-making exercise.

Despite more liberal times, the divisions both within the USA (where censorship of the arts in general is still rife) and social rules and mores in other parts of the world still make obvious movie censorship in Hollywood inevitable if sales are to be maximised worldwide.

When topics such as LGBT+ and particularly trans identities are addressed in major studio films, they are done in the least provocative way, lest it limit an otherwise great story's success.

In the popular James Bond feature No Time to Die (2021) Ben Wishaw as Q is interrupted by Bond as he prepares for a romantic dinner at home with another man, but we never see Q's date and the dinner is the only reference to his sexuality. Wishaw, who is gay himself, told Rolling Stone magazine that he considered raising the issue: "Maybe on another kind of project I would have done? But it's a very big machine. I thought a lot about whether I should question it. Finally, I didn't."

It is also not unusual for big films to have special editions palatable for countries where liberal norms - gay relationships, nudity, ridicule of government or religious figures – are not readily embraced. For example, the version of Bohemian Rhapsody (2018) released in China had all scenes removed which showed Freddie Mercury's sexuality and any reference to him being with another man expurgated. This had a profound effect on the entirety of the film's narrative – much more than when Kate Winslet's bare breasts were edited out of Titanic (1997), also for the Chinese market.

The Hollywood dream machine could, in theory, make any film it wants to and yet it seems to favour remaking the same films. Last year eight of Hollywood's highest grossing films were remakes, reboots or based on a known brand. This year's retreads include Mean Girls, Mad Max's Furiosa, Planet of the Apes and Ghostbusters.

The fact is, Hollywood has no lack →

## Military precision

....................................................................................................................

**DAISY RUDDOCK on a surprising relationship**

THE IDEA THAT the US Department of Defence (DoD) directly influences Hollywood storylines sounds like it should be a state secret, a revelation covertly whispered off the record alongside a "you didn't hear this from me".

However, it's actually an open fact – one that the DoD doesn't just accept but promotes.

Its website boasts of having worked with filmmakers in Hollywood for more than a century and the Pentagon even has its own Entertainment Liaison Office.

The department says that this is simply to ensure that depictions of military stories are "accurate", admitting that it "reviews a rough cut of a film, so officials can decide if there are areas that need to be addressed before a film is released".

But Debra Ramsay, a senior lecturer in film studies at the University of Exeter, in the UK, calls the term "accuracy" in this context a "minefield".

"Accuracy is often about which narratives institutions like the DoD choose to invest in, and which they don't," she said.

As such, although it stresses that its priority is the correct portrayals of the military, the DoD's obvious lack of objectivity raises questions. When the department put heavy pressure on the makers of the 1997 James Bond film Tomorrow Never Dies to take out a reference to the failure of US forces in Vietnam, officials were clearly more preoccupied with preserving the reputation of the US Army than correcting technical terms.

However, Ramsay also points out that filmmakers have the power to decide how far government interference goes, citing producer Darryl Zanuck as an example.

"When making The Longest Day, [Zanuck] was co-operating with the US military but refused to agree to cutting a scene where American GIs shoot two German soldiers who have their hands up and are saying 'Bitte, bitte', which means 'Please, please' in German.

"The military could not control whether or not that scene made the final cut."

Accusations have been made that DoD-endorsed films such as Top Gun: Maverick (2022) amount to military propaganda – the original 1986 film caused a spike in army recruitment – but Ramsay points out that filmmakers aren't forced into pushing this message, arguing that it's less a "sinister arrangement" and more an "opportunity for positive publicity".

There is, of course, the possibility that filmmakers have engaged in self-censorship in order to garner favour with the military for help with their films, but this is difficult to prove.

The very notion of the US government being involved in creating media opens up clear avenues for censorship, but the extent to which these avenues are being taken is much harder to assess.

**Daisy Ruddock** is editorial assistant at Index

CREDIT: Gabe via Unsplash

→ of unique, entertaining or innovative screenplays – and it has those on tap: a hoard of unmade scripts made famous by Franklin Leonard's Black List of "most-liked" screenplays which were never developed.

But since the days of risky studio-busting, director-driven disasters such as Michael Cimino's 1980 flop Heaven's Gate – it's understandable that the Hollywood money men prefer a safe bet.

When Hollywood's decisions go right, we have a swell of interest in cinema, in the red carpet, in actors – and often in the film's message, whether it is there overtly or not.

Hollywood's biggest potential rival, China, is only able to make what appear to be poor reproductions. Home Coming (2022), set in the fictional North African country of Numia and based on the 2011 evacuation of thousands of Chinese nationals from Libya ahead of the civil war, did well domestically, but grossed far less worldwide than the US film Top Gun: Maverick released the same year.

Independent, documentary, short and experimental filmmakers abound in the USA. They can make perfectly good – sometimes great – films on a much lower budget. Yet they will rarely attract the attention of larger distributors.

Hence, personal films or those of a more controversial bent might be made with smaller budgets and distributed with specialist streaming services such as Mubi where they can reach an audience more or less as their creators intended but they're not seen by vast numbers.

There are great stories that aren't being told, but social norms change. US writer Amy Heckering's 2008 remark that, "Hollywood is the dream factory, and no one dreams about older women," is being overturned by the success of films like The Idea of You (2024), starring Anne Hathaway, as a 40-year-old woman who

## Censorship in Hollywood

**A brief history by DAISY RUDDOCK**

THE US FILM industry is a dominant force not only in global cinema but in society itself, having been credited for shaping much of western culture. Many groups have attempted to capitalise on this influence over the years by regulating content to further their own agendas, and Hollywood has therefore struggled against censorship for much of its history.

When films began to grow in popularity in the USA in the early 20th century, the Supreme Court ruled that the right to free speech outlined in the US constitution did not apply to movies, sparking a nationwide movement to censor them. This led to the creation of the Motion Picture Association of America (MPAA), which was led by politician and Presbyterianism Church member William Hays.

Moral clauses were introduced into actors' contracts, creating a blacklist within the film industry. However, it was the creation of the Motion Picture Production Code in 1930 – known commonly as the Hays Code – that was the biggest barrier to free expression in film.

The Hays Code was a set of rules Hollywood films were expected to adhere to in order to make their content "safe". Certain topics or themes were censored, such as sexually explicit content and swearing. Even more concerning was the strict emphasis the rules placed on family values, which was used as a guise to prohibit homosexual and inter-racial

relationships from being shown on screen.

Some filmmakers ignored the code. To combat this, in 1934, the Production Code Administration (PCA) was created.

Led by Catholic layman Joseph Breen, this administration had to approve all movies produced in Hollywood prior to their release, introducing a ratings system for the first time and forcing studios to abide by the morality rules.

Studios self-censored, avoiding topics that might invoke the ire of the PCA. Others would send their scripts off only for them to be returned with the dreaded "condemned" rating, meaning changes would have to be made.

Although the code lost its influence in the early 1960s and was eventually quietly disbanded for good in 1967, much of the damage had been done.

Conservative patterns within filmmaking during this era – the erasure of Brick's homosexuality in the film adaption of Cat on a Hot Tin Roof, for example – have been normalised, banishing certain themes to subtext long after the code has gone.

The current system of ratings is more relaxed, but producers are sometimes forced to edit their films to avoid the highest rating – NC-17 – which would make theatres reluctant to screen them. The legacy of censorship is a difficult one to shake.

***Daisy Ruddock*** *is editorial assistant at Index*

falls in love with a man 15 years younger.

As with other activities, film and TV is at the front line of changing social preferences. With that, the American narrative is slowly shifting with its audience's wants and tolerances.

Then there is the growing influence of Netflix, which has made more films more available to people. As a successful

UK-based Hollywood producer puts it: "Netflix have been a brutal catalyst, and now occupy a dominant position in the market, but Hollywood of old is a tough old dog and is reconsidering how to reset their traditional business model into something more suited to latest technology and audience expectations." ✖

*Karen Krizanovich is a freelance film journalist and film concept researcher. Additional reporting by **Sally Gimson***

53(02):48/50|DOI:10.1177/03064220241274929

## It's understandable that the Hollywood money men prefer a safe bet

LEFT: Saudi Crown Prince Mohammed bin Salman tours the Neom Centre for Knowledge Enrichment

SPECIAL REPORT ◆ THE FINAL CUT

# Strings attached

**JP O'MALLEY** looks at how Saudia Arabia has gone from having no cinemas to being at the heart of the modern film industry

WADJDA (2012) TELLS the story of a 10-year-old Saudi girl who dreams of buying a bicycle. Directed by Haifaa al-Mansour, the film set three cultural historical precedents upon its release 12 years ago.

It was the first Saudi feature film to be shot entirely in Saudi Arabia, the first feature-length film made by a female Saudi director, and the first film Saudi Arabia submitted for an Academy Award consideration.

Alas, there was no Oscar. But the film had a lasting cultural impact.

Sarah Taibah was in her early 20s, studying for a master's degree in fine art in San Francisco when she first watched it at the cinema.

"I cried," the 35-year-old artist, actor, writer and filmmaker explained from her home in Jeddah.

Taibah had good reason to be emotional. Cinema was then still banned in the conservative kingdom. The ban begun during the 1980s, when conservative Islamists introduced it. The first film to be shown in public after it was lifted in 2018 was American superhero tale Black Panther.

The first Saudi film to be screened in public was Rollem (2019), which Taibah starred in.

At that stage, Saudis were making films on YouTube, she said. "We were the number one content makers for YouTube for many years and we made many films here before there was cinema."

Taibah is a celebrity in Saudi Arabia and has appeared on the covers of Marie Claire Arabia and Vogue Arabia. Her rise to fame coincided with the success of dark comedy Jameel Jeddan (2022), broadcast on Shahid, the world's leading Arabic streaming platform, facilitated by Saudi state broadcaster MBC.

The show set another cultural historical precedent – Taibah, its creator, became the first Saudi woman to write and star in her own TV show.

She is part of a new generation of Saudi filmmakers. Modern, suave and cosmopolitan, most earned their cultural credentials in the West.

There are limited freedoms in Saudi Arabia today, said Taibah – "especially when it comes to topics like sex".

But subtlety can work to a filmmaker's advantage, she said. "There are many ways to show intimacy on screen which allow space to imagine and respect the audience."

Riyadh-based director Khalid Fahad agrees.

"People in Saudia Arabia don't like to see sexual scenes [in movies], so when we talk about [censorship] it's not about rules and regulations, or about the government, but about respecting the culture and the audience," he said.

His films, including Valley Road (2022) and From the Ashes (2024), are currently available on Netflix. Fahad, who studied film in Canada, the UK and the USA, said the cinema ban in Saudi Arabia was often misunderstood.

"The ban was specific: watching film in public places," he said. "It was not ➜

 ## Individuals in Saudi Arabia know if they are critical of the authorities they are likely to face harsh sentences

→ a ban on watching movies at home. There were shops in Saudi Arabia where you could rent DVDs and markets where you could buy them."

Fahad claimed the Saudi authorities implemented the ban because there were not many films being made at the time and they were concerned that showing international movies in a communal public space that did not relate to Saudi culture or heritage "might change people's religious beliefs".

Today, the film industry in Saudi Arabia is booming, with accumulative box office revenues (mostly from Hollywood blockbusters) hitting almost $1billion since cinemas reopened.

Those figures are from an article published in March in British film magazine Screen Daily. It's a sponsored feature piece, paid for by the Saudi Film Commission.

Set up in 2020 and affiliated with the Saudi Ministry of Culture, the commission is ambitious.

It believes the country will eventually have the capacity to compete with the Egyptian film industry, Bollywood and European cinema.

"This will take time," said Fahad.

The country has only a small number of feature films made by Saudi directors but he said it was the top ranking country in the Middle East for cinema ticket sales.

And he mentioned the recent success of Norah, directed by Saudi filmmaker Tawfik Alzaidi which received a Special Mention from the jury at this year's Cannes Film Festival.

"The Saudi Film Commission has been very supportive of Norah and contributed a lot of the budget for promoting the film at this year's Cannes Film Festival," said a spokesperson for TwentyOne Entertainment, a film acquisition and distribution company based in Riyadh.

It's no secret that the commission has deep pockets and is more than willing to flash the cash for cultural projects.

At the moment it's offering international filmmakers lucrative incentives to shoot films there – but getting US and British filmmakers to speak on the record about working in Saudi Arabia proves difficult.

One filmmaker, currently working on a film that was shot in Saudi Arabia did agree to an interview with Index. But they were not granted the approved authority needed from the Saudi Ministry of Culture, which also happens to be the main funder.

Mohamed Ghazala, an assistant professor of animation and the chair of the Cinematic Arts School at Effat University in Jeddah, said the ministry was now "looking at cinema as another economic resource as Saudi Arabia moves to diversify its income away from industries other than oil".

He also spoke about the delicate issue of censorship.

"Saudi film makers know they live in a conservative society, so they have their

## Shut up and take the money

SALLY GIMSON finds out more about politics, power and movies in Saudi Arabia

WHEN MAHMOUD AL-MASSAD was offered $40,000 from the Red Sea International Film Festival fund to finish his new documentary, Cinema Kawakeb, he was overjoyed. He needed money for post-production and sources of funding for documentaries in Jordan are limited.

But then he was sent the contract.

"To my surprise ... it said I am not allowed to criticise Saudi Arabia in any format on social media or publicly," he told Index.

"What is so silly [is that it said] I can't do this until 2030."

Al-Massad asked fellow filmmakers and discovered this was normal practice.

He joked: "Maybe on 1 January 2030 I will publish all my cursing on social media [saved up] for the past six years!"

He rejected the money on principle.

"You have to be really honest with yourself as a journalist or filmmaker. You

can't do something about humanity when someone has already bought your freedom and dignity," he said.

Saudi Arabia is doling out hundreds of millions of US dollars, and many filmmakers have swallowed their consciences to take it.

Most of the legal dealings are carried out in secret, but Saudi Arabia's censorship emerged into the open at last year's Red Sea festival.

It was held in the first week of December, only months after the start of the Israel-Hamas war.

Other film festivals in the region had been cancelled and organisers scaled back events in solidarity with the Palestinians. But Saudi Arabia's Ministry of Culture was having none of it, went ahead with the film festival and refused to stop other activities which were part of its planned five months of parties and celebrations aimed at making Riyadh "the Middle East's new centre of entertainment,

sports, live events and incredible cultural and dining experiences".

Palestinian and other filmmakers hoped they could raise the Palestinian cause at the festival but found themselves gagged. Middle East Eye reported festival-goers were banned from wearing the Keffiyeh (the Palestinian scarf) and al-Massad told Index even people wearing tiny Palestinian flag pins were prevented from going into screenings.

The event was star-studded, with many Hollywood legends attending – including Gwyneth Paltrow, Johnny Depp, Halle Berry and Andrew Garfield.

The jury was chaired by celebrated Hollywood director Baz Luhrmann with actors and directors from around the world.

Although nothing political could be said about Palestine, Palestinian films were awarded prizes and funding.

Al-Massad told Index some Palestinian

CREDIT: UPI Photo /Alexis C. Glenn / Alamy

own self-censorship," he said. "They don't focus on the authorities but on how Saudi society will perceive their films."

The Saudi film scholar, author and director said all international film makers and companies going to work in the country "welcomed, but with an appreciation of the local culture and community rules and ethics, set by the Ministry of Culture".

This is something Netflix understands. "There is compromise between what Netflix wants for [its audience] and what the Saudi [authorities] are willing to accept," Ghazala said.

In January 2019, several Western media outlets reported that Netflix withdrew an episode of the comedy show Patriot Act with Hasan Minhaj, after Saudi officials complained.

The episode of the news-comedy programme in question raised the issue of Jamal Khashoggi. The dissident Saudi journalist, who wrote for The Washington Post and was critical of Saudi

# The ban was specific: watching film in public places

Crown Prince Mohammed bin Salman, was murdered in the Saudi consulate in Istanbul in 2018. US intelligence agencies have since claimed the Crown Prince approved the assassination.

In February, Vanity Fair ran an article exploring Hollywood actor Johnny Depp's close cultural and financial ties with Saudi Arabia.

In the same month, The Hollywood Reporter published an article about how The Red Sea Film Foundation (a non-profit organisation created to support the film industry in Saudi Arabia) has approved financial backing to Modi, an upcoming biopic – mostly shot in Budapest – about the life of Italian artist Amedeo Modigliani, starring Al Pacino and directed and produced by Depp.

Bissan Fakih, Amnesty International's campaigner for Saudi Arabia, said getting famous actors to speak in a positive manner about the country was a way for it to project an image to the world that human rights had improved.

"Amnesty has not come across any cases of individuals in Saudi Arabia who are being detained for making films or documentaries," she said. "But there is a zero-tolerance policy for criticism inside Saudi Arabia right now, which is the worst that we as an organisation have ever documented for freedom of expression."

Fakih said there might be some situations where the Saudi authorities would allow filmmakers a little more freedom but added: "It would be very difficult to produce a film or a  →

filmmakers were so angry that they couldn't raise the Gazan cause they returned the Saudi money – but couldn't talk about it publicly because of the contracts they had signed. Others kept their funding and have been feted this spring in Cannes.

Not everything about Saudi Arabia's involvement in film is bad, al-Massad told Index.

He is very supportive of young Saudi filmmakers and describes holding a film workshop in Jeddah before the controversy – "one of the best" he has ever done.

"Two short films from the workshop have been screened on Netflix – something I'm proud of," he said. "Saudis are amazing people and [there is] such a variety of people in Jeddah. It was fascinating."

Al-Massad has joint Dutch/Jordanian citizenship and is no stranger to censorship in his country of birth. His feature film Blessed Benefit, from 2016, cannot be shown in

Jordan, even though it was one of the first Arab films to be screened on Netflix, where it is still available.

The Jordanian government objected to scenes where public officials and police officers were bribed, even though it is now commonplace because of the high cost of living and low wages.

He is amazed that in the USA he has received money from the Sundance Festival "to make a film to criticise [US] policy and politics", but added: "It's wonderful!"

He is continuing to work on his new documentary, Cinema Kawakeb, about an old deserted cinema in Amman bearing witness to the city.

"Now," he said, "I want to work on a good film, I want the least money possible, and I want to be happy. This is the most important thing."

*Sally Gimson* is acting editor at Index

ABOVE: Cinematographer Mahmoud al-Massad at the Sundance Film Festival

# Hooray for Saudiwood: Is moviewashing the next big play?

**MARK STIMPSON** reports on the money Saudi Arabia is investing in the film industry around the world

IT IS NOW more than a century since Hollywood's emergence as the centre of worldwide film production. Studios were attracted to Los Angeles by the sun, the low cost of land and easy access to a variety of locations. It was also easier for studios in LA to avoid the gaze of Thomas Edison's Motion Picture Patents Company on the other side of the USA in New Jersey.

Now Saudi Arabia is trying to do the same – and some of the reasons why early producers went west are now attracting them eastwards.

Saudi has sun in spades: Jeddah is one of the hottest places in the world.

It also has land – plenty of it – which can easily be repurposed without worrying about the objections of those who have lived on it for generations, as is the case of the half-trillion-dollar Neom project for a new urban area in Tabuk which has displaced the Huwaiti tribe (Index vol 52,3 p12).

Money, though, is the big attraction and Saudi has plenty of it, which it is using to extend its soft power globally.

Oil money has gushed into sport by the gallon in the last few years, particularly in football and golf, and now it is the movie industry's turn.

At the Cannes Film Festival in 2022, the country announced details of a film tax incentive scheme that would allow productions to claw back 40% of their in-country spend in cash.

Tax schemes such as this can work well, and other countries have already proven this. Fiji offers producers incentives of 47%, Poland 50%, rising to 70% for "difficult films".

The controversial Neom project is at the heart of the country's burgeoning movie sector and there are two production facilities based nearby – Media Village and Bajdah Desert Studios.

Media Village currently has two 2,500 square metre sound stages as well as workshops, production offices and make-up and green rooms. Two more stages are already under construction on the same site. Bajdah Desert Studios has two 3,000 square metre soundstages and four more are planned.

The Neom site also has accommodation for cast and crew and five-star hotel rooms for the on-screen talent.

Dunki, directed by Rajkumar Hirani and starring Shah Rukh Khan, is the first Bollywood film to shoot at the facilities in Neom. It will not be the last.

Neom is also central to plans for MBC Studios, the production arm of Middle East broadcaster MBC Group, which recently moved its HQ to Riyadh.

At the 2023 Red Sea International Film Festival, the studio's then managing director – former US TV executive Christina Wayne – said the company was "making a push to shoot a large part of our slate in Saudi Arabia".

However, she lasted only just over a year in the role. In March 2024, the Hollywood news service Deadline reported that she resigned because "she is unable to move to Saudi Arabia full-time".

MBC Studios is behind the movie Hwjn, directed by Yasir Alyasiri, and the $120 million-budget Anthony Mackie movie Desert Warrior, shot at Neom.

Jeremy Bolt, a producer on the film, gives a testimonial on the Neom website, saying: "At Neom, we are not reliant on CGI because it's a real oasis, surrounded by the most phenomenal mountain desert landscape I've ever seen."

Saudi Arabia provided the backdrop for the Gerard Butler action flick Kandahar, by director Ric Roman Waugh, which in 2021 became the biggest Hollywood feature to shoot entirely in the country.

A year after announcing tax breaks, the Saudi Ministry of Culture returned to Cannes to announce the launch of two separate film sector funds worth a total of $180 million. The money was intended to both develop the movie industry inside the country and, more importantly, attract productions to go there.

At the time, it was announced the schemes were aimed at productions which feature the kingdom's "culture, history and people along with showcasing the kingdom's diverse selection of landscapes".

The $100 million Saudi Film Fund, launched in February, is intended "to spur investment in this industry" and is a collaboration between the Cultural Development Fund, MEFIC Capital, which will manage the fund, and ROAA Media Ventures.

ROAA will be the technical partner and will seek "to facilitate collaboration with leading international studios and create content that highlights Saudi culture and values".

Tellingly, the chairman of ROAA is Redha Alhaidar, former president of the General Commission of Audiovisual Media, the Saudi media regulator.

The Saudis' other film incentive fund is the Red Sea Fund, which has granted $15 million in support to more than 250 films.

The fund is also aimed at projects from directors of African nationality as well as those of Arab nationality or origin.

The 2023 movies Omen, written and directed by Belgian-Congolese director Baloji, and Goodbye Julia, directed by Sudanese director Mohamed Kordofani, have both received investment from the fund.

As detailed elsewhere in this issue, countries with deep pockets recognise the power of movies to extend influence around the world. After all, Hollywood has been doing it for years.

*Mark Stimpson is associate editor at Index*

→ documentary without the agreement of the Saudi authorities.

"There is also self-censorship, because individuals in Saudi Arabia know if they are critical of the authorities they are likely to face harsh sentences."

The cinema market in Saudi Arabia is expected to reach $1.70 billion by 2030. It seems, for now at least, that actors and filmmakers from across the world are willing to look the other way at ongoing human rights abuses. Money talks. And profit will dominate most of that global conversation." ✖

*JP O'Malley is a freelance journalist*

53(02):51/54|DOI:10.1177/03064220241274930

# Filmmakers pull it out of the bag

Film professor **SHOHINI CHAUDHURI** explores some of the innovative strategies employed by Iran's filmmakers to circumvent censorship

N A PERCEPTIVE video essay titled Irani Bag, made in 2020, Maryam Tafakory illustrates how Iranian filmmakers get around the Islamic taboo on touch. Interweaving her commentary with film clips from 1989 to 2018, she highlights how bags have long been a recurring device in Iranian films, allowing men and women to "touch" on screen.

In one clip, a man and a woman riding on a motorbike are separated – or connected – by a bag lying between them. It functions as a substitute for human touch or an object of shared intimacy.

A bag can also be an extension of the body, and Tafakory demonstrates how men and women in these scenes repeatedly push, pull or strike each other using bags.

By contrast, in the scenes she shows without a bag, hands hover centimetres away from another person – the actors forbidden from touching.

If no direct contact materialises on screen, the filmmaker can dodge censorship. And, as Tafakory shows, Iranian cinema has developed a cinematic language "to touch without touching".

Touch is not the only prohibition in Iranian cinema. The government has sought to align cinema and other arts with its interpretation of Islamic principles, and an overarching rule is gender segregation, which prevents men and women who are not *mahram* (related by blood or marriage) from interacting with each other.

As part of this, the wearing of the veil in public is strictly policed, as witnessed by Mahsa Jina Amini's police custody death in 2022 and the ensuing →

BELOW: Jafar Panahi stars as a taxi driver in his docufiction Taxi Tehran, which he also directed

LEFT: Iranian director Rakhshan Banietemad had to work around constraints of gender segregation in her 1995 film The Blue Veiled

imposed constraints. This is reminiscent of Hollywood under the Production Code from 1934 to 1966 when political, religious and cultural restrictions on filmmaking compelled directors to employ subtle techniques that left more to viewers' imaginations.

In Iranian cinema in the 1980s and 1990s, it was noticeable how often key roles were given to children. This was partly a creative response to new taboos as, in the early decades of the Islamic Republic, filmmakers realised that children could overcome constraints of gender segregation by acting as adult substitutes or purifiers of male-female contact.

For example, when the protagonist Nobar shares intimate moments with her lover Rasul in The Blue Veiled (1995), her youngest sibling, Senobar, serves as a mediator. Senobar even rests her head in Rasul's lap, a proxy for her sister. The child lends an innocent aura to an erotically charged scene.

Children can also cross social boundaries and navigate between private and public spaces. In Jafar Panahi's debut feature The White Balloon (1995), a little girl, Razieh, embarks on a quest to buy a goldfish for Nowruz (Persian New Year) and encounters people from different walks of life on Tehran's streets,

→ Woman, Life, Freedom protests. Since cinema is regarded as a public space, female characters are always expected to be veiled – even indoors with their families where they would not wear veils in real life.

Cinema is regulated by the Ministry of Culture and Islamic Guidance (MCIG). Directors must submit their synopsis or screenplay for a production permit and, later, their completed film for a screening permit. At each stage they can be asked to make changes or otherwise risk censorship. When a film is released, the Iranian press can accuse the makers of *siāh-namāyi*: presenting the country in a negative light.

There are some obvious red lines for the censors: no direct criticism of Islam or Iran's Islamic Republic, nothing

too violent, and certainly no sex. But MCIG guidelines are not detailed, so moviemakers have learned other censorship criteria through trial and error.

What is permissible is always shifting due to changes in society and filmmakers pushing against boundaries.

It is important to observe that state censorship is not the only obstacle that Iranian filmmakers encounter. International funders and markets impose expectations of what their films should be about. Indeed, many filmmakers have reported to me that they find these restrictions to be as challenging as censorship.

But where censorship is concerned, filmmakers who want to explore intimacy and other sensitive topics must find creative ways to work around

## Since cinema is regarded as a public space, female characters are always expected to be veiled

including an Afghan balloon seller.

Filmmakers have subtly used children to highlight Iran's sociopolitical realities, among them the after-effects of the Iran-Iraq war (as in the 1989 film Bashu, the Little Stranger), the plight of the country's Afghan minorities (The White Balloon) and the Kurds' hardships on the Iran-Iraq border (for example, A Time for Drunken Horses from 2000, or 2004's Turtles Can Fly).

The political climate has waxed and waned as moderate and hardline governments have relaxed censorship restrictions and tightened them again. Yet intermediaries for male-female contact have been enduring ploys throughout.

In one of several storylines in Tehran: City of Love (2018), a woman called Mina dates a man, Reza, who ultimately confesses he is married. As consolation, he couriers her a giant teddy bear. Subsequently, Mina is seen waiting at a bus shelter side-by-side with the gargantuan soft toy – Reza's comic stand-in.

Another creative solution has been the use of the road movie genre. Simultaneously private and public, a car is a space that allows small, everyday transgressions. Being in a car relaxes the rules of compulsory veiling and encourages behaviour normally kept behind closed doors. It emboldens people to express themselves more freely. Filmmakers tap its emancipatory potential in both their production strategies and their on-screen representations.

In Ten (2002), a female passenger, whose fiancé has jilted her, removes her headscarf to reveal her head shaved in mourning and as a token of a new beginning. In Panahi's Taxi Tehran (2015) – his third feature made clandestinely since his 2010 filmmaking ban – a series of passengers take a taxi. The cabbie is Panahi himself, masquerading in a beret. Before his ban, he was accustomed to filming in the bustling outdoors. With the car and small digital cameras, he can shoot outside again.

One of his passengers is lawyer

Nasrin Sotoudeh, renowned for her work defending political prisoners. Like Panahi, she has been repeatedly imprisoned and banned from leaving Iran and practising her profession. As she gets out, she advises him to delete her words from his film to avoid more hassle from authorities. This is an underground film – made illegally, without official permits, and distributed on Iran's black market and abroad. So Sotoudeh's words survive the edit, registering the film's furtive mode of production.

In Atomic Heart (2015), we first encounter Arineh and Nobahar intoxicated after a party. They are part of a modern, Westernised subculture that likes to revel, drink and take drugs, and largely rejects the Islamic Republic's values. As their anti-regime attitude cannot be directly shown, the film hints at their unconventional lifestyle by inhabiting the road movie genre – associated with freedom and rebellion – as they whirl around nocturnal Tehran. The film evokes the subversive behaviour of real-life Iranian youth who, given restrictions on public gathering as well as bans on nightclubs and disapproval of open displays of romantic affection, have taken to the highways, especially at night.

Inserting a story within a story is a further tactic for circumventing censorship. In The Salesman (2016), Emad and Rana perform Arthur Miller's Death of a Salesman in an amateur theatre group. The film mirrors the play, highlighting the couple's relationship after Rana is assaulted by an intruder in their apartment – a scene left unshown to avoid censorship and engage the audience in speculating about what transpired between Rana and her attacker. In the story within a story, meaning is multi-layered, residing in the inner as well as the outer tale.

Since short films are less strictly regulated by screening permit requirements, directors are bypassing these rules by composing feature films from several shorts. Mohammad

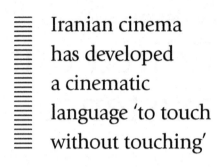

## Iranian cinema has developed a cinematic language 'to touch without touching'

Rasoulof's There Is No Evil (2020) comprises four short stories about characters involved in the state's capital punishment system. Given Rasoulof's filmmaking ban, his production team tactically applied for four short film permits without listing his name on the forms.

In Tales (2014), which was also created as multiple shorts joined together as a feature, a documentary filmmaker character shoots a film within a film. When an official notices his camera filming a workers' protest, the recording halts. The film segues to the next story, suggesting the camera's confiscation. Later, the filmmaker retrieves his camera without the seized footage. He determines to continue filming, stating: "No film will ever stay in the closet. Someday, somehow, whether we're here or not, these films will be shown." His words reflect a popular Iranian saying that a film's purpose is to be shown to an audience.

These kinds of strategies are testament to Iranian filmmakers' creativity. Although they cannot be overtly critical of the regime, they have developed resourceful ways to try to ensure that their films can explore sensitive topics and still be shown. ✖

*Shohini Chaudhuri is a professor in the Literature, Film and Theatre Studies department at the University of Essex, and author of Crisis Cinema in the Middle East: Creativity and Constraint in Iran and the Arab World (Bloomsbury, 2022)*

53(02):55/57|DOI:10.1177/03064220241274931

# Edited out of existence

Queer people are being written out of Nollywood or, at best, being misrepresented, writes **TILÉWA KAZEEM**

FOR A LONG time, Nollywood – the Nigerian film industry – has mirrored the country's homophobic shadow. Frame by frame, it has narrated stories depicting daily biases and struggles, but often stereotyping and stigmatising queer characters.

When queer characters first appeared in Nigerian cinema, they were portrayed within narratives that vilified, demonised and labelled them as "sinful".

Some films which exemplify this trend are Emotional Crack (2003), which explored the relationship between a married woman and a vengeful bisexual; Beautiful Faces (2004), which depicted lesbians as dangerous; and Men in Love (2010), where the main character is drugged and raped by his long-time friend and business partner for rejecting his advances, only to succumb following what can be described as a "conversion" assault. Unlike in major powerhouses such as Hollywood, where LGBT+ individuals are depicted with nuance, Nollywood directors often knew little about queer experiences. These films aimed to guilt closeted individuals into changing and reiterated the belief that being gay was abnormal and sinful. The National Film and Video Censors Board did not object, as such movies were seen as educational content.

"The Nigerian government, particularly the Censors Board, has used its power to suppress queer-themed movies and stories, deeming them 'immoral' and 'unacceptable'. This censorship is rooted in discriminatory

laws and a conservative culture that perpetuates harmful stereotypes and marginalisation of queer individuals," queer actor and artist Babatunde Tribe told Index.

The Same-Sex Marriage Prohibition Act during President Goodluck Jonathan's administration was the final nail in the coffin, criminalising same-sex marriage and punishing it with a 14-year prison sentence. Since then, queer characters have faded into obscurity in Nigerian cinema. With their presentation effectively dead, young storytellers keen on sharing their experiences have sought external assistance or undertaken these projects themselves

Kayode Timileyin, the documentarian behind On The Streets, which spotlights the struggles of trans-feminine people in Lagos, explains that funding was a significant challenge.

"The entire documentary was shot with $5,000, which was less than enough," he said. "So, a huge part of the film was funded out-of-pocket, gathering funds here and there, and paying street thugs to [film] peacefully so they don't smash our cameras and equipment."

Making a queer documentary in Nigeria presents unique security risks. Filmmakers often navigate dangerous environments where individuals weaponise the law against queer people. In Timileyin's case, there was no scenario where the thugs would leave without being paid off. Calling the police would have been like jumping from the frying pan into the fire.

ABOVE: A still from Babatunde Apalowo's award-winning film All The Colours Of The World Are Between Black And White

Casting is a further significant challenge. Securing actors willing to take on queer roles in such a conservative society is difficult. Director Babatunde Apalowo, known for his award-winning film All The Colours of the World Are Between Black and White (2023), which depicts the affectionate relationship between the two main characters, Bawa (Riyo David) and Bambino (Tope Tedela), revealed that he almost abandoned the project after actors withdrew at the last minute.

Echoing similar challenges, queer filmmaker Wapah Kelechi Ezeigwe faced hurdles in casting for the short romantic drama Country Love (2022) – a coming-of-age tale set in Enugu about a man returning home after 15 years.

Ezeigwe said that some actors (but not all) suggested changes to intimate scenes, saying: "I think the problem may lie in how these actors want you to tweak the story in places they feel are too much for a character."

This reluctance, even if subtle, is partly due to the subject matter.

The inescapable atmosphere of homophobia infiltrating the industry has seeped into the foundation of storytelling, stifling creativity and imagination while frustrating the efforts of those bold enough to create queer characters. Since these films exist as personal projects rather than mainstream Nollywood productions, they fail to push the needle towards meaningful change.

Within Nollywood, such narratives are often deemed unworthy of disrupting the delicate status quo. The stigma surrounding the subject matter and the fear of becoming a target also hinder the possibility of a revolution.

Additionally, major streaming platforms such as Netflix and Prime Video, known for promoting LGBT+ content in the West, understand the delicacy of the situation and are cautious about investments. However, South African streaming service Showmax walks a tightrope between accurately ➤

These films aimed to guilt closeted individuals into changing

→ depicting queerness in Nigeria and avoiding a ban.

The TV series Wura is the longest-running series to feature queer characters in Nollywood. The Showmax original centres around Wura (Scarlet Gomez), a mother and CEO of a gold mining company. Her closeted gay son Lolu (Iremide Adeoye) grapples with keeping a hidden romantic relationship with Femi (Oluwaseyi Akinsola), a young gay man, while simultaneously dating a woman his family is eager for him to marry.

The series is an adaptation of the South African telenovela The River, and offers a respectable depiction of what it means to be a gay man in an unaccepting culture such as Nigeria.

However, its shortcomings are equally glaring. The producers deliberately avoid showing any form of romantic or sexual gestures between the characters as, given the current climate around same-sex relationships, this approach helps the show avoid legal scrutiny and reflects Nollywood's tentative progress towards acknowledging diverse sexualities.

But while it explores the struggle between societal rejection and self-acceptance – a stage Hollywood has long moved past – it still perpetuates the stereotype of queer individuals as societal abominations. By shrouding the affection with cut scenes and ambiguity, it ultimately makes these characters reductive and simplistic.

In 2018, US actress Scarlett Johansson stepped down from portraying a transgender man after public backlash. Critics argued that casting cisgender actors in transgender roles deprives marginalised communities of opportunities. Despite progress in Hollywood, similar challenges persist in Nollywood, hindering authentic queer representation.

The director of the Wura, Rogers Ofime, described the casting process as arduous, saying he aimed to avoid stereotypes about queer men and their appearance or mannerisms. He

# For some queer individuals, seeing straight actors play queer characters can feel like mockery or appropriation

highlighted the actors' commitment to understanding their roles, fostering believable on-screen chemistry through intimate gestures such as holding hands.

Meanwhile, Tribe, who began their career as a queer actor in 2017, described the journey of queer actors in Nollywood as "challenging and largely invisible".

They explained that, historically, queer roles have been scarce, and many queer actors have faced discrimination and marginalisation within the industry. Although there has been a recent push towards greater representation and authenticity in casting, the practice of casting straight actors in queer roles can perpetuate the erasure of genuine queer voices and experiences. Tribe believes it is crucial to consider the broader context and the potential impact on the queer community.

Tribe said that while authentic representation was essential, the influence of storytelling and the impact of queer characters on audiences should also be recognised, noting: "For some queer individuals, seeing straight actors play queer characters can feel like mockery or appropriation, particularly if the portrayal is stereotypical, inaccurate or exploitative. It is vital to prioritise sensitivity, respect and authenticity in these portrayals."

Ezeigwe takes a broader view, addressing not just the issue of representation but also the depth and significance of queer characters in Nigerian cinema, arguing that many filmmakers view inclusion as a trend rather than a genuine commitment to diversity.

This approach, Ezeigwe suggests, results in a superficial portrayal of queer existence, making it seem watered down and unfamiliar. They emphasise the importance of meaningful character

development. Tokenistic inclusion, they argue, undermines the genuineness and richness of queer experiences on screen.

When Apalowo created All The Colours of The World Are Between Black and White, he honoured a friend who was lynched because of his sexuality. Despite being straight, he created well-layered characters that beautifully depicted queer life in Nigeria. Art is most appreciated when there is a profound connection between the creator and the work. Creating queer characters should follow the same principle, crafted with sincerity to resonate with the people they represent.

Although it is easier said than done, any meaningful change in Nollywood would require it to open its doors to queer filmmakers to tell their stories authentically. This includes allowing queer inclusion in roles or, at the very least, consulting with community members to achieve accurate representation.

Without such changes, storytellers such as Ezeigwe and Apalowo will continue to seek external support to tell stories that, if nurtured within the country, could spark change and promote inclusivity.

They aren't holding their breath for drastic change, but with the help of young, queer Nigerian filmmakers they aim to reshape perceptions, showing that queer characters are not a trend. Queer inclusion is not about playing woke; it is critical, deliberate and an effort to substantively centre queer characters and let them drive the story from beginning to end. ✖

*Tiléwa Kazeem is a Nigerian sex columnist with an interest in culture stories*

53(02):58/60|DOI:10.1177/03064220241274933

# LETTERS FROM LUKASHENKA'S PRISONERS

**Exhibit Launch: 5 August, 7pm**
St John's Church, Waterloo, SE1 8TY

This image is taken from a letter sent from prison by Maksim Znak,
a lawyer and former member of democratic leader Sviatlana Tsikhanouskaya's team.
He has been behind bars since September 2020.

CREDIT: Photo 12 / Alamy

LEFT: 2006 film Summer Palace caused trouble between director Lou Ye and the Chinese authorities

SPECIAL REPORT ◆ THE FINAL CUT

# Making movies to rule the world

**JEMIMAH STEINFELD** talks to author **ERICH SCHWARTZEL** about the global influence of the Chinese film industry

MY FIRST PROPER experience of Chinese propaganda was served to me in a UK cinema courtesy of a US film. The year was 2006 and the film in question was Mission: Impossible III, one of the highest grossing of the year.

With the assistance of the China Film Co-production Corporation and the China Film Group Corporation, it featured the skyscrapers of Shanghai's Pudong, all shimmer and shine and neon lights, which Tom Cruise scaled before dashing off to a nearby ancient water town – quaint and idyllic. A few months later I was standing before the film's sites and the reality was different. To be sure, Shanghai's neighbouring water towns are quaint. Idyllic? Perhaps. And the Pudong skyline really is exciting, especially at night. It's just that out of the film's shot, and very much in real-life focus, was the poverty, the honking cars, the cranes. It was not all perfect.

I tell this anecdote to Erich Schwartzel, author of Red Carpet: Hollywood, China, and the Global Battle for Cultural Supremacy, and he's unsurprised.

"You start to watch American movies and if there's ever a scene or plot that detours into China you start to notice all of these considerations," he said.

Law, order, modernity – these are all front and centre when it comes to films set in, or from, China. A morass of deals and promises goes into filming any scene to ensure that it remains on message, reckons Schwartzel – a morass that is exhausting and has now turned many studios off filming there. This would be a good thing, but it simply means we are now just getting less stuff from China, rather than more honest stuff.

For decades, China has been using the film industry to tell its story – or rather to tell the Chinese Communist Party (CCP) story. And Hollywood executives, actors, directors, producers and others in the business have largely been going along with it.

In addition to the airbrushing, they've removed scenes, they've changed dialogue and they've avoided certain topics entirely, all to appease the CCP. I tell Schwartzel about a book on the Tiananmen Square protests and massacre that I was disappointed hadn't been turned into a film, and he said he often heard such a line – of something that would work perfectly on the silver screen, only it would cause too much trouble. The mind boggles to think how many films have not been made.

## Beijing plots

Schwartzel's book, which was published in 2022, was born of his many years reporting on the film industry for The Wall Street Journal. He took up the post in 2013, arguably just the right time to monitor the China market. While the country was no stranger to cinema – Shanghai's film industry was a major player in the interwar period, for example – China had been largely closed to Western movies under Mao Zedong. This started to change in 1994, when a deal was made for Hollywood to send 10 movies a year to the country. This was then raised in 2012 to 34 foreign films.

Schwartzel had a sense that, from the get-go, China was going to shake up Hollywood. He explains a Hollywood tradition of "dumb money" – investors who are made to feel important and good, but essentially lose money – and how he'd attended more than one "surreal" event in Hollywood where an anonymous Chinese billionaire would be held up as the new money in town.

The hope was that they'd play a similar, hands-off role to those investors of before. But there were two critical differences, Schwartzel said. The first was China's huge and increasingly middle-class population (the economic rise of China translated into box office hits that could gross $1 billion by 2020, as opposed to the more humble $3 million from 1994).

Then there was the more critical element. It had, said Schwartzel, "a regime that was defining itself as an alternative to Western liberal democracy and no medium did more to spread Western liberal democracy around the world than the film".

"So you had this real corrupting of this medium by a regime that appeared to be pretty focused on doing it themselves and trying to exercise their own soft power abroad," he added.

In addition to the carrot – offering access to the world's biggest movie market – which saw a flourishing of co-productions such as Kung Fu Panda 3, Matt Damon's box office flop The Great Wall and the Oscar-winning Green Book, China used the stick to keep Hollywood in line. The country would (and still does) regularly boycott actors for previous roles or statements that were critical of China. When Hong Kong streets were filled with protesters as part of the 2014 Umbrella Movement, for example, actors who joined in faced various boycotts in China and were even dropped by their own.

In a message posted on his Sina Weibo account, Hong Kong film director Wong Jing declared that he was "unfriending" the actor Chapman To.

"We have worked well together in the past and I respect your right to hold your own political views. But I absolutely do not agree. To avoid embarrassment, your contact details will be erased from my phone and my computer. Have a happy life," he wrote.

Beijing also exploited other vulnerabilities. "All of the major studios are owned by much larger conglomerates that have other exposures to China, so whether it's supply chain issues with merchandise or whether it's trying to get other movies into the country or operating a theme park there, there are a number of ways that the Chinese government has economically punished people for messages or messaging that they don't approve of," Schwartzel noted.

## Soft power fail?

But Chinese censors might be victims of their own success. While no politically hard-hitting films enter the China market from Hollywood, no major hard-hitting films leave the country either. That's not to say brave directors don't exist within China. In 2006, for example, the film Summer Palace was released.

Directed by Lou Ye, it dared to cross that bright red line of Tiananmen. Unsurprisingly, the film brought Lou into conflict with the authorities. After it was screened at the 2006 Cannes Film Festival without government approval, Summer Palace was placed under a de facto ban in China, and both Lou and his producer were not allowed to make films for five years. That didn't stop him. In 2018, The Shadow Play premiered in Taiwan. It dealt with forced evictions and featured Hong Kong actor Edison Chen. This year at Cannes he screened his latest project, An Unfinished Film, which takes place in a hotel near Wuhan in January 2020.

Lou might be one of the bravest directors to come out of China today. On a less confrontational level, as Schwartzel points out, there are also those who will try to "push the envelope as much as they can – so they might have a character that is coded gay or be about more conspicuous consumption".

Still, when it comes to soft power through film, China is simply not winning, and part of the reason must lie in censorship, as opposed to other factors such as language. Consider neighbouring South Korea: it has had the kinds of soft power hits – in shows, films and music – that Beijing would love. "There is no world in which Chinese moviemakers are able to make Squid Game and Parasite," said Schwartzel. "The movies and TV shows that are made in China and then approved to be shipped out of China are the most sanctioned movies and TV shows that they make."

China has though made remarkable inroads into some African countries and is now the biggest trading partner on the continent. Part of its investment is in film. They now have film festivals, such as the China-Africa International Film Festival held in Cape Town in 2017 and the China Kenya Film Festival in Nairobi last year.

Successful film partnerships include Wolf Warrior 2 – described by Lin Songtian, the Chinese ambassador in →

No medium did more to spread Western liberal democracy around the world than the film

→ South Africa, as "an excellent Chinese film that carries forward patriotic enthusiasm and friendship between China and Africa". Co-productions involving African actors and filmmakers are less sure-footed. The recent My African Bride (2022) is a romcom about an African woman (exact country unspecified) and her new Chinese husband. In the opening scenes of the movie, the husband has painted his face black ostensibly so that his wife doesn't stand out when they are travelling on the bus. Another African/Chinese romance movie Black Tea (2024), directed by Mauritanian filmmaker Abderrahmane Sissako, was panned in the South China Morning Post for its "tone-deaf representation of the African diaspora's experience in the country".

Schwartzel said he went to one small town in Kenya that had a cinema showing so many Chinese movies that the man who ran it was nicknamed Bruce Lee. Typically, though, it's in people's homes where most people watch kung fu movies and Chinese films dubbed into English and African languages including Swahili and Yoruba. These are shown on the very cheap StarTimes satellite

.....................................................................

BELOW: The Shanghai skyline that was showcased in 2006 film Mission: Impossible III

service – part of a huge infrastructure project to bring digital TV to Africa, sponsored by Chinese president Xi Jinping. So successful has it been that by 2027 StarTimes is set to be the second-largest pay TV provider in Africa, with a subscriber base of 12.6 million.

## Final twists

While most people living outside China are not won over by Chinese movies, people in China are now less won over by Hollywood movies – and that has changed the terms of engagement.

As Schwartzel says: "The market in China is really turned off from Hollywood films now. It's very rare for Hollywood movies to make anywhere near the amount of money they used to."

This means it's a lot easier for US studios to walk away. Schwartzel points to two high-profile cases of Hollywood saying "no" to China. The first was the furore over Tom Cruise's jacket in the revamped Top Gun. In the original movie it had the Taiwan flag on it. The patch was removed in the new one out of fear of a backlash from Beijing, only to be reinstated in case of a bigger backlash from US audiences. In the last Spider-Man movie that Sony released, a scene that took place at the Statue of Liberty was asked to be cut by Chinese

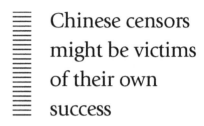

# Chinese censors might be victims of their own success

censors, which the studio refused to do.

"I don't think that was a brave act of patriotism. The Chinese market was already such an uncertainty and the executives behind the film knew that they would have a public relations nightmare on their hands if word got out that they had, indeed, cut a scene featuring the Statue of Liberty to appease CCP censors," said Schwartzel.

This is all well and good, but has the damage already been done?

"China had come to Hollywood with a mission that it has largely fulfilled," Schwartzel said when I asked him who comes out best in his book. He's clear – it's China.

"I think there are elements of the book that China doesn't like to see in print, but at the same time there is an undeniable pride in China about how quickly they have mounted this massive industry."

China has created a blueprint for other countries seeking influence on the global stage, such as Saudi Arabia. Films are being used as vehicles to sanitise that country's image to the world and Hollywood-supported film festivals and stars are heading there to serve as de facto ambassadors. As Schwartzel says, it's indicative of the state of global geopolitics today.

Hollywood was about how the USA told its story to the world when it reigned supreme. Today it doesn't. So what is the sequel to US supremacy? China, Saudi Arabia and a host of others would like you to buy a ticket to their next film and see. ✖

*Jemimah Steinfeld is CEO at Index*

.....................................................................

53(02):62/64|DOI:10.1177/03064220241274934

# When the original is better than the remake

**SALIL TRIPATHI** says even Bollywood is being captured by a Hindu nationalist narrative

N A FILM with a convoluted, improbable plot of the kind only Bollywood directors are capable of, the 1977 Hindi blockbuster Amar Akbar Anthony told the story of three brothers, separated at birth. In the film, a wealthy man kills someone by mistake and asks his driver to take the rap, promising that his children will be looked after. When he is released from jail, the driver finds his family starving. When he confronts his boss, goons are set on him. He flees and hides his children in a park, near a statue of India's founding father, Mohandas Gandhi.

The oldest son is saved and adopted by a Hindu policeman. A Muslim tailor adopts the second and the third, who goes to sleep near a church, is adopted by priests and brought up as a Christian.

One day, the brothers are called to

ABOVE: A protest against Amazon Prime series 'Tandav' takes place in India

a hospital to donate blood for an ailing woman. They don't know it, but she is their mother. The three men lie on different beds, their blood being taken and merged, flowing together to revive their mother.

"You don't get India unless you have Amar, Akbar, Anthony, blood and blood, paying their debt to the motherland," the Indian novelist Jerry Pinto wrote, while recounting this film, in a volume of writings I co-edited in 2022 about India at 75.

I used to say that the trope of three brothers separated at birth and reunited at the end was Hindi cinema's way of thinking about Pakistan and Bangladesh. That we don't make these films any →

ABOVE: 2019 film The Surgical Strike

→ more is perhaps our way of reconciling to the new political reality of the subcontinent. When Pinto showed the film to students recently, one of them asked if Akbar was circumcised by his Muslim father, and if Anthony remained a Christian or had returned to the Hindu fold. On bad days, Pinto wrote, he knew the answer; on days of hope, he clung to the promise in the film's title song:

*Anhonee ko honee kar de, honee ko anhonee.*

*Ek jagah jab jamaa ho teenon:*
Amar, Akbar, Anthony
When the three are together, they make the impossible possible.

That was the spirit of Bollywood.

In the 1959 Hindi film *Dhool ka Phool* (Flowers of the Dust) there is a moving, emotional song – *tu Hindu banaga na musalman banega, insaan ki aulad hai insaan banega* (You won't become a Hindu, nor a Muslim; you are the child of a human being, and a human being you shall be).

The song has a lilting melody, is haunting and quaintly nostalgic and, given the charged relations between Hindus and Muslims in India today, is oddly mawkish.

While Hindus and Muslims built the Indian film industry together – the earliest directors and filmmakers came from all faiths and languages – communal undertones were ever-present. Mumtaz Jehan Begum Dehlavi, once the highest-paid movie star in India, had to adopt a Hindu name – Madhubala – to gain acceptance, just as Mohammed Yusuf Khan had to take a Hindu name, Dilip Kumar, so that his career could thrive in newly-independent India. That changed towards the turn of the last century and, in recent years, three of Bollywood's biggest stars have been Shah Rukh Khan, Salman Khan and Aamir Khan.

The late Irrfan Khan, Nawazuddin Siddiqui, Saif Ali Khan and his daughter Sara Ali Khan never felt it necessary to change their names, as if indicating the new confidence, swagger and acceptance of stars with Muslim names on India's silver screen.

But India has changed in the last quarter of a century. After Hindu fundamentalists destroyed the Babri Masjid mosque in 1992, the country has lurched in a different direction, moving away from its secular ethos. While Prime Minister Narendra Modi suffered a setback in the most recent election, losing 63 seats and no longer commanding a majority in parliament, the fact remains that his Bharatiya Janata Party (BJP) won more than twice the seats of its nearest rival, Congress.

In this changed landscape – the BJP does not have a single Muslim member of parliament – life has changed for Muslims. They find it hard to rent or buy property in mixed or Hindu areas, aren't given permission to expand their mosques and are attacked if they pray in public. Petty humiliations against Muslims are routine.

Instead of rallying round the vulnerable, some Bollywood filmmakers have become enablers of hate. As if

## Bollywood's journey began with a rich tradition of mixing faiths

suffering from amnesia about its inclusive past, Bollywood has produced a series of films in recent years which are unabashedly pro-establishment, parroting the Hindu nationalist narrative.

India hasn't had a formal census since 2011, but a quarter of India's 1.4 billion people are under the age of 14. Influencing that generation is the major preoccupation for the BJP. And to do so, the party is relying on catchy slogans, peppy songs, attractive memes and viral messages on the internet. Along with swanky malls, quicker trains, bridges and highways, monuments such as the world's largest cricket stadium and a vast temple on the site where the destroyed mosque once stood, Modi has been busy remaking India.

It is in that context that these films become important. One recent film called India's premier academic institution – Jawaharlal Nehru University – Jehangir National University, giving the university named after India's first prime minister a Mughal emperor's name.

Another celebrated Vinayak Damodar Savarkar, who coined the term Hindutva and was arrested (but acquitted) in the conspiracy to assassinate India's founding father. Neither did well at the box office, showing that Indians prefer entertainment to propaganda.

Earlier, The Kerala Story manufactured statistics and treated as truth unverifiable assertions made on social media suggesting that many Indian Muslims had joined Isis.

And The Kashmir Files was a gory, exaggerated account of atrocities committed against Kashmiri Pandits (who are Hindu by faith) by Islamic separatists, completely ignoring the brutal treatment of Muslims in Indian-held Kashmir by troops.

Two more films rewrite the recent past. In Accident or Conspiracy, Godhra crafts a different narrative about the circumstances that led to the 2002 killings in which more than 1,000 people were massacred – the large majority of them Muslims – in retaliation for the burning of

a train in which 59 Hindu activists died.

Sabarmati Report, which is on the same subject, will be released in August 2024. Both films are significant because Modi was Gujarat's chief minister at the time, and he was accused of incompetence in failing to prevent the violence, if not of complicity.

He warmly praised Article 370, a film that essentially justified the abrogation of the provision in the Indian constitution which granted the former state of Jammu and Kashmir a special status. Many such films are exempt from entertainment tax to boost their box office figures, and government employees are given a day off to see the film – they get paid if they show the ticket stub that proves they've seen it.

These films were timed to coincide with the recent elections. Major production companies were involved, and the films openly supported Modi and targeted rival politicians.

There have been other films, too – a 2019 film, Uri: The Surgical Strike, showed the army taking retaliatory action against Pakistan after a terrorist attack. And in another form of the weaponisation of Bollywood, films involving Aamir Khan, who has often spoken out in defence of India's secular character, have been boycotted.

BJP activists have succeeded in getting streaming services such as Amazon Prime to apologise for a show, Tandav, for denigrating Hindu deities, and Netflix to remove the film Annapoorani because it showed a Hindu woman eating meat and a Muslim man explaining the complexities of Ramayana and its treatment of food.

Bollywood's journey began with a rich tradition of mixing faiths, where narratives often transcended religious and political divides to emphasise unity and diversity. Films such as Mother India (1957) and Mughal-e-Azam (1960) celebrate India's cultural diversity and interwoven tapestry, portraying characters from diverse backgrounds with empathy and understanding. These

ABOVE: Salman Khan (left) and Aamir Khan (right) are two of Bollywood's biggest stars

movies epitomise the secular fabric of India, where communal harmony and coexistence were cherished values.

The intention of the overt hypernationalism, the vilification of minorities, and the crafting of a chronicle that glorifies Hindu fundamentalism is to reorientate the thinking of younger Indians. The rise of social media and digital marketing has further amplified this phenomenon, allowing producers to target specific demographics and capitalise on existing political sentiments.

As Bollywood grapples with the shifting ideological alignments, the need to assert that old outlook has become more acute. Producers – particularly streaming platforms not beholden to the Indian state – must reassert their autonomy instead of kowtowing to the vociferous minority which claims to represent the majority and silences movies that speak of inclusion.

India is now a different country, facing a multitude of challenges. The tragic decline of its once-inclusive cinema may appear small, but as the medium that united the "multi-everything" country at one time, its embrace of right-wing nationalism weakens its appeal and cheapens its worth. ✖

*Salil Tripathi is Index's South Asia contributing editor*

53(02):65/67|DOI:10.1177/03064220241274936

# Selected screenings

**MARIA SORENSEN** speaks to filmmaker **VITALY MANSKY**, who is committed to truth and freedom. When it comes to Russia, sometimes that means not showing films at all

THE LAST TIME I saw Vitaly Mansky, he was presenting his documentary Putin's Witnesses, detailing the Russian leader's rise to power, at Zurich Film Festival in 2018.

It feels like a different era. Navalny was alive and there was no full-scale war of aggression by Russia against Ukraine. This was before the emergence of Belarus's opposition leader Sviatlana Tsikhanouskaya, the protests which rocked the country and the massive repression that followed.

Born in Western Ukraine and having moved to Moscow in the 1980s, Mansky is now one of the top internationally recognised documentary filmmakers. His films have been shown at more than a thousand festivals worldwide and won numerous awards. In 2007 he founded Artdocfest in Russia, an independent documentary festival that quickly became a unique space for challenging the state's domination of the media. It provided a showcase for films dedicated to topics either entirely absent or misrepresented in the Russian loyalist media.

He last tried to hold Artdocfest in Moscow in March 2022, just after the start of the war, when he was harassed and sprayed with paint by those reported in the press as activists from an ultranationalist movement.

It had been clear for some time, he says, that the festival could never remain free, civilised, open and uncensored in Russia and after the annexation of Crimea, he brought the main festival to the Latvian capital where he had moved, and it became Artdocfest Riga. For a few years he showed the main programming

in Latvia and then screened some of the films in Russia, censorship permitting, but after the full-scale Russian invasion of Ukraine, Mansky completely withdrew.

Now the festival exists as an independent, international documentary film festival in Riga and the programming has become even edgier. Artdocfest also travels to various cities in Central Asian countries (except Turkmenistan), to the states of the former Soviet Union, the Eastern Bloc, even to the "old" Europe. Last year it had screenings in Paris which were very well received and the plan is to continue next year. The festival also supports the films with direct funding, especially those from undemocratic countries.

I ask him first how the international community can show solidarity and support.

"Solidarity, above all, is providing the screens to those films that reflect the tragic reality in countries with authoritarian regimes," he says.

"That is to say, you have to understand that there are people who continue to record the reality that is happening in a warring country and try to tell about the nature, the roots, the consequences of these crimes, and they do it at their own risk. They do it really risking their lives and their freedom, their own and their loved ones."

I ask about calls to boycott Russian culture, which in itself is a complicated topic. Artdocfest has a rule that films produced by state studios in Russia and Belarus will not be shown, but filmmakers who have left their countries and do not accept current circumstances

will be featured.

What does Mansky think about the "no good Russians" discourse. Why are some Ukrainians against sharing a platform with all Russians?

"You know, as far as Ukrainians are concerned, it's a completely separate story, he says. "And I am in solidarity with my Ukrainian colleagues who find it difficult to be physically present in the same space with people from Russia, because of the crimes and the grief, the losses that Ukrainians suffer every day at home as a result of Russian aggression. This gives them not just the right to intolerance but it requires our understanding of it, which is sometimes considered excessive. But it is not excessive, it is a natural, understandable reaction to the pain.

"And when an opera theatre in Ukraine removes Swan Lake from the repertoire, for example, I see it as an

LEFT: A still from Mansky's 2018 documentary, Putin's Witnesses

I ask him what this means in practice.

"This is, of course, a certain restriction of rights and it causes certain difficulties in everyday life, difficulties in communication. While working I have to take the role of an anonymous participant in some processes that we still influence, so as not to cause problems for people who still live and work in Russia. It's a set of problems that make it impossible to enter the country, to do anything in the country. It's one of the instruments of applying pressure."

The body of Mansky's work is very diverse. He and his camera had a close look at the first three presidents of the Russian Federation in the trilogy Gorbachev: After Empire (2001), Yeltsin. Another Life (2001), and Putin, the Leap Year (2001). He addressed the collective Soviet generational traumas in Private Chronicles. Monologue (1999). He filmed the lack of freedom under communist rule in Cuba in *Patria o Muerte* (Motherland or Death) (2011). He travelled along the Trans-Siberian gas pipeline by car in *Truba* (Pipeline) (2013). He showed the reality of the totalitarian propaganda machine in North Korea by filming undercover when invited there for an official visit in Under the Sun (2015).

What attracts him to these themes and close looks at authoritarianism, authoritarian countries and systems?

"It's not so much films about Cuba and North Korea as countries, it's more about freedom and unfreedom, about a society of people who have lost their freedom, a society of people who don't understand the value of freedom."

He explains that the same principle guides his latest work:  →

appropriate, natural and understandable gesture. After all, when Russia is forbidden to use the Russian anthem at international competitions, they use Tchaikovsky's concerto as the anthem of a warring country."

But he draws a distinction when it comes to Russian culture outside Ukraine and Russia itself: "When it comes to La Scala or America, other European capitals, here I would [like to] see a more reasonable and more sober understanding and approach to these issues. In the civilised world, the state does not dictate or regulate cultural policy.

"In a free society, the right to make decisions is in the hands of those people who have earned the right to curate festivals, theatres, exhibitions ..., and it is a matter of using their sense of adequacy, balance, fairness and so on when they make a decision.

"In other words, the boycott of

Russian culture is an understandable thing. Boycott in general and sanctions in the broad sense of the word, economic, political, and cultural is an understandable and adequate thing but balance and common sense is required."

In September 2022, Mansky was put on a federal wanted list by the Russian authorities. At the same time, a criminal defamation case was initiated by pro-Kremlin film director and Moscow International Film Festival president Nikita Mikhalkov. The same year, the Kremlin declared Mansky a "foreign agent" for his opposition to the war in Ukraine.

It's not so much films about Cuba and North Korea as countries, it's more about freedom and unfreedom

CREDIT: Everett Collection Inc / Alamy

LEFT: Director Vitaly Mansky believes documentary films should be used to spur democratic countries into action

→ "I am, both as a human and as an author, worried about the acceptance and normalisation of the war, its slow penetration and weaving in our everyday lives. That's why in my latest documentary I am looking at exactly these aspects.

The film I am shooting now is about this war entering our peaceful lives and our bloodstream. This contamination of blood with war, with militarisation in a healthy person who as a result becomes sick and more susceptible to external influences and also weaker, so to speak."

I tell Mansky that maybe it's impossible to absorb it all the time. You wake up, you read and read, and then you start to take care of yourself and your mental health.

He tells me about a near-death experience while shooting Pipeline: "At night, we were filming in the north, the heating went out in the car we were sleeping in. I remember how I started to realise in my sleep that I was freezing, but it happens in a dream, and you can't wake yourself up in a dream. Because you are cold, you want to hide from this external pain, the cold, and to shrink and to go deep into this dream. And if you don't wake yourself up…." His words trail off. "I miraculously woke myself up, I saved myself from death and the three people who were in the car with me by making myself wake up.

"European civilised society must force itself to wake up otherwise it will perish in its sleep. This sleep is like death for us, not for Ukraine. Ukraine is not sleeping, it is fighting, day and night. That's the problem."

I ask about Russian society. After Navalny's death "I believe that the question of saving Russian society is not relevant now. Now it is necessary to help Ukraine win the war. This is the main issue on the agenda now. When Ukraine defends itself and wins, or when a ceasefire acceptable to Ukraine is signed, then maybe we should think about what should be done in Russia, with Russia."

Mansky is currently working on two films in Latvia while promoting his latest documentary, Eastern Front, which was co-directed with the Ukrainian filmmaker Yevhen Titarenko and follows a brigade of volunteer paramedics who work directly in the war zone, providing a graphic depiction of the drastic consequences of Russian aggression in Ukraine.

I ask him if there is a future for filmmaking and art in general in Russia.

"I have a rather radical position here," he says. "I think Russia is a completely unfree country, and I don't believe that it is possible for a free artist to exist in Russia today and to realise their artistic projects, if the state knows about it. And it is quite difficult to do any artistic projects without the state knowing about it. It is possible, but difficult. Therefore, I believe that Russia is doomed now to create alternative underground art, *samizdat* and so on, like in the Soviet years or to develop controlled official art, which in one way or another will be a compromise and that is a very slippery slope in times of war."

Mansky sees the role of a documentary filmmaker in waking society up whenever it falls into dogmatic slumber. That it is still possible for him to continue making and producing films despite all the obstacles is an inspiring testament of resilience. ✖

*Maria Sorensen is a Belarusian writer based in Switzerland*

53(02):68/70|DOI:10.1177/03064220241274938

 European civilised society must force itself to wake up otherwise it will perish in its sleep

CREDIT: Keystone Press / Alamy

# A chronicle of censorship

**MARTIN BRIGHT** reports on how a TV giant in the USA is preventing a documentary film about the Babyn Yar massacre being shown

THE BABYN YAR massacre is one of the bloodiest atrocities in Ukraine's dark history. In late September 1941, 33,771 Jewish residents of Kyiv were herded by the Nazis into a ravine ("Babi Yar" in Russian, "Babyn Yar" in Ukrainian) on the outskirts of the city. Over a two-day period, the victims were shot and buried in mass graves as part of what became known as "the Holocaust of Bullets".

Oleg Chorny's small-budget feature documentary From Babi Yar to Freedom tells the story of the massacre through the lens of Soviet defector and writer Anatoly Kuznetsov, who first revealed the full scale of the atrocity to the world when he escaped to the UK in 1969. The film was completed in 2017, five years before Russia's full-scale invasion of Ukraine, and is an extraordinary tribute to Kuznetsov's determination to tell the truth in the face of a wall of Soviet censorship and disinformation.

Chorny's documentary deserves a wide international audience, but in an irony that would not be lost on the dissidents of the 1960s, no one can see it because of a rights dispute over the central archive interview in the film owned by the giant US TV corporation CBS.

In July 1969, shortly after Kuznetsov defected, he gave a lengthy interview to the veteran CBS news journalist Morley Safer in which he opened up about his decision to escape the Soviet Union. Kuznetsov went to London, accompanied by a KGB minder, to research the time Lenin had spent there in 1903, and secretly took with him film containing the text of the full version of his book Babi Yar: A Document in the Form of a Novel, stitched into his clothing. The book is based on eyewitness accounts of the massacre and Kuznetsov's own boyhood diary.

Now, Chorny has been told that nine minutes of CBS footage from the Kuznetsov interview (freely available →

LEFT: Russian author Anatoly Kuznetsov in 1969

# Chorny has been told that nine minutes of CBS footage from the Kuznetsov interview will cost $80,000

→ on YouTube) will cost $80,000 – more than the budget of the movie. Wazee Digital, a Colorado-based asset management company which negotiates on behalf of CBS, has refused to budge on this fee.

Chorny told Index that the fate of the film and the fate of Kuznetsov were intertwined in his mind. "I'm sorry, you must understand that the story with this film is a sad story for me because it was not released… But if something happened and this movie was released, I think it would be so important, because nothing has changed from these times with the KGB. You can call it the FSB, but it does not matter."

In the documentary, Chorny follows Ukrainian writer Stanislav Tsalyk as he tracks down traces of Kuznetsov – who died in 1979 – in Kyiv and then in London. Tsalyk travels to the UK with Kuznetsov's son Olexiy, who remained in the Soviet Union. In one of the most moving scenes, Olexiy stands next to his father's unmarked grave in Highgate Cemetery. Olexiy, too, has now died without seeing the film released.

The story of Kuznetsov is a classic Cold War tale, but it is much more than that. It is a story about how stories themselves are told, how they can be misrepresented, and how they are suppressed.

Kuznetsov's Babi Yar has had many lives and suffered multiple rounds of censorship. When it was first published in the Soviet Union

in 1966, the censor made cuts that underplayed the suffering of the Jews. In the Soviet narrative, Babi Yar was known as a Nazi act of horror against Soviet citizens. The Jews of Kyiv were thus doubly erased: once literally and then historically. This was not all that was removed from the original text: references to cannibalism during the Ukrainian famine, the Holodomor, where millions died as a direct result of Stalin's policies, and parallels between

fascism and communism were all excised. Anything, in fact, that showed the Soviets as less than heroic.

The whole uncensored version is recognised as a singular masterpiece. The first chapter, Ashes, begins: "This book contains nothing but the truth." The typefaces of the book reveal its troubled publication history, with the original text in plain type, previously censored passages rendered in bold, and later additions from Kuznetsov in square brackets.

ABOVE: Documentary footage shows a mass grave being covered after the Babi Yar massacre

Oddly, this adds to the experience of reading Babi Yar. Its fragmented text suits the battered and broken subject matter.

Take the following passage about Dina Pronicheva, a 30-year-old puppet-theatre actor and survivor of the massacre who later gave evidence against the Nazis. "Dina went across the hillock and sat down. Everybody there was silent, crazed with fright. *She was afraid to look up: somebody might recognise her, quite by chance, and cry out: 'She's a dirty Jewess!' These people would stop at nothing to save their own skins. For that reason she tried not to look at anybody, and nobody looked at her.* Only an old woman sitting next to her in a fluffy knitted scarf complained quietly to Dina that she had been seeing her daughter-in-law off and had got caught... *But she herself was a Ukrainian, she was no Jewess, and whoever thought it would come to this?* They had all been seeing people off."

The censored words in bold give the episode a very different meaning and emotional impact.

When Babi Yar was republished in a Vintage Classics edition in the UK last year under the title Babi Yar: The Story of Ukraine's Holocaust, it didn't receive the attention it deserved.

When I talked to Chorny in Kyiv over Zoom, I suggested that this latest episode in the story of the massacre is part of a pattern. I said: "Even if you go back to the origins of the story... This is a story about silence. It's a story about censorship. It's a story about not being able to tell the story and so..."

Chorny stopped me and said my interpretation did not go far enough: "Excuse me, this is a story of a totalitarian system which is the same as the Nazi totalitarian system. And this is a story of resistance – Anatoly Kuznetsov's personal resistance, I mean: to escape to publish the full version in the West." Josephine Burton of Dash Arts has been pushing for the release of Chorny's film since 2021, when her organisation began work on Songs of Babyn Yar, a music and theatre project that used Kuznetsov's text in the production. Burton, who also championed the cause of the Crimean Tatars in Dash Arts' 2022 performance Crimea 5am, told Index: "Oleg Chorny's documentary needs to be seen. It tells a remarkable story, a vital contribution to the history of Ukraine and the Holocaust.

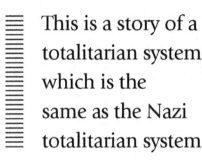

# This is a story of a totalitarian system which is the same as the Nazi totalitarian system

This film should not be silenced."

Chorny has also gained the support of the Koffler Centre in Toronto, which ran a series of events about the Babyn Yar massacre last year, including a Zoom discussion with Chorny and his team.

In the meantime, Chorny describes life in Kyiv: "We are living some kind of surrealistic reality. This is mixed with news from the front from our colleagues and friends. A lot of losses. Especially in the last year, we buried a lot of friends and some colleagues who disappeared on the front line."

But the director has kept himself busy. Chorny has made a short film, Kyiv in the Days of War, about the aftermath of the Russian attacks in 2022, and three 15-minute films in a series about creativity and the Ukraine conflict: Art in the Land of War. In one of these, If I Stop It Means They Win, sculptor and graphic artist Oleksandr Smyrnov says: "I think that if they prevent me from doing what I'm good at and what I want to do, then they have won. That's why I'll keep doing it."

Two years ago, an appeal to raise money for a headstone for Kuznetsov in Highgate cemetery raised more than $1,300. In another twist in the story, his surviving daughter has not given her permission for it to be erected. The best memorial would be the release of From Babi Yar to Freedom. [CBS was approached for a comment on this story.]. ✖

*Martin Bright is editor-at-large at Index*

53(02):71/73|DOI:10.1177/03064220241274939

# Erdoğan's crucible

While two of Turkey's most prominent filmmakers are stuck in prison **KAYA GENÇ** talks to journalist and filmmaker **FIRAT YÜCEL** about whether the tide is turning, what films can be made today and the influence of his dissident actor father

TO THE DELIGHT of many, at the end of March, Turkey's strongman president Recep Tayyip Erdoğan received the biggest thrashing of his political career. His populist Islamist party, the AKP, came second in the local elections for the first time in its 23-year history. Eighteen days later, as I attended a film screening at the International Istanbul Film Festival, the sense of optimism was palpable in the crowded cinema. It seemed Turkey was on the brink of getting rid of the most repressive political leader in its recent history.

One immediate outcome of Erdoğan's stunning electoral defeat was the apparent relaxation of cultural censorship. Hold Still, a harrowing film about the struggle of a Kurdish family whose children were kidnapped, tortured and buried in a well by Turkish security forces in 1995, won the festival's best documentary prize. Such an outcome would have been unlikely in the wake of another Erdoğan victory.

Over the past decade, which has been among the darkest eras in terms of freedom of expression in Turkey, people who produced political films →

RIGHT: Fırat Yücel and his colleague Senem Aytaç call for the freedom of persecuted filmmaker Çiğdem Mater

A film that was never made

...esulted in an 18 year prison sentence in ...rkey for film producer **Çiğdem Mater**

I didn't make a movie about the Gezi Park protests, but I might as well have done it. The place to talk about this is movie theaters, not courtrooms. **"**

Çiğdem Mater

...eÇiğdemMater

→ were relentlessly prosecuted by Erdoğan's autocratic regime. That is why the seeming relaxation of Turkey's censorship machine came as a surprise.

An event at the same festival half a decade ago marked the apotheosis of Turkish censorship. In April 2015, it cancelled the screening of the documentary Bakur. Filmmakers Çayan Demirel and Ertuğrul Mavioğlu spent months with Kurdish militants to document their lives. But before the screening, the Ministry of Culture intervened and argued that Bakur didn't have a licence.

That censorship brought together directors whose films were scheduled to run at the festival. Twenty-two films were withdrawn. The closing ceremony was cancelled. The festival's widely respected director, Azize Tan, who was at the helm of the event for nine years, spoke out against censorship in a press briefing. A few months after the kerfuffle, she resigned from her post. Jury members, film directors and critics joined a boycott. The Palme d'Or-winning director Nuri Bilge Ceylan, as well as staff of the film magazine Altyazı, were among the boycotters.

Fırat Yücel, a founding editor of Altyazı, was in the Netherlands when Hold Still, produced by former Altyazı editor Enis Köstepen, received the festival's top prize. Yücel and Köstepen were fellow students at Istanbul's Bosphorus University, which boasts a long history of leftist activism, when they founded the magazine in 2001. Altyazı ceased print publication in 2019 (it continues as an online-only magazine), but Altyazı Fasikül: Free Cinema, a spinoff that focuses on freedom of expression in cinema, increasingly became the primary source of news for Turkey's film communities as

Erdoğan's assault on culture intensified.

While editing Altyazı Fasikül, Yücel became an even more passionate anti-censorship activist and filmmaker. Altyazı Fasikül's primary purpose, according to its website, is to increase the visibility of the works of filmmakers who face risks of government repression and censorship.

Yücel and his colleagues organise screenings of films by directors and collectives who are at risk, and try to ensure Altyazı Fasikül provides a safe platform for under-represented and censored filmmakers.

Last year, Yücel fell victim to censorship when he sent Translating Ulysses, a film he co-directed with Aylin Kuryel, to the International Istanbul Film Festival for consideration in its 2023 programme. Organisers told Yücel and Kuryel that while they liked the film, which tells the century-long suppression of the Kurdish language in Turkey, they couldn't "show it under the current pre-election conditions in Turkey".

Yücel said the festival organisers were trying to minimise the risks. "They wielded their power of censorship in our case, calculating that they could relax it if the opposition triumphed in the May 2023 presidential elections."

Yet Erdoğan won that election. Shortly afterwards, he attended an opening with the directors of the Istanbul Foundation for Culture and Arts (İKSV), which organises the festival. Cameras showed Erdoğan's entourage joking and chatting away with the İKSV's leaders.

For Yücel, cases of political censorship of films rooted in the self-interest of Turkish tycoons are nothing new. He knows about its persistence from his family. Yücel's father was the legendary film actor Erkan Yücel, who starred in a flurry of masterpieces of

Turkey's political cinema, including Yılmaz Güney's Anxiety (1974) and Erden Kıral's On Fertile Lands (1980).

The latter film debuted a day after the military coup of 12 September 1980. It was screened for just one week before the military junta banned it. The Ministry of Culture at the time tried to stop the jury of a major film festival in Turkey from awarding the film its top prize.

When On Fertile Lands reached fame in Europe and won a prize in Paris, the film's crew could not leave Turkey to receive the accolade. Their passports were confiscated. Finally, the prize jury travelled to Istanbul to present the award to Kıral, the film's director. But Turkish intelligence officers trailed the film's crew and blocked them from receiving it. The negative of On Fertile Lands then disappeared for years. (It re-emerged in the 2000s and a restored copy was screened in 2008.)

Yücel is proud of his father's political legacy as a participant in some of the most aggressively banned productions in Turkey's film history. Erkan Yücel was arrested multiple times, tortured in captivity and spent years in jail. His death in a car accident in 1985 traumatised Yücel. "I only came to appreciate his political legacy when I reached my 30s," he said.

Yücel describes the generation who grew up after the 1980 coup as unwillingly depoliticised. He was no different. "I was raised in a way that protected me from politics," he recalled. But at Bosphorus University, Yücel began appreciating his father's practice. Films and politics, he saw, were not separate realms, and films need not be confined to cinemas. Instead, "they could be distributed to workers and the underprivileged through factories and college campuses".

His father wanted political cinema to trespass boundaries. "He travelled through Kurdish cities in Anatolia. He stepped on tractors to stage plays. He was detained multiple times for these activities, yet he remained consistently unyielding."

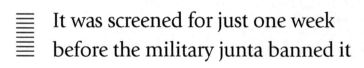

## It was screened for just one week before the military junta banned it

Yücel said these tactics inspired his democratic struggle. "I didn't experience torture or imprisonment myself. But I approached filmmaking as something adjacent to political organising like my father did."

Yücel began editing Altyazı in 2001. From that time to 2013, when thousands of anti-government protesters filled Turkey's squares during the Occupy Gezi protests, Yücel watched the slow brewing of a culture of dissent.

First came "video activists" who documented protesters marching against the privatisation of public spaces or at rallies against the Iraq War. Then film buffs started organising. Many joined a grassroots movement to save Emek, a historic cinema in Istanbul. "The Emek is ours, Istanbul is ours!" was the collective's slogan.

Yücel was one of the group's most active participants. He appreciated the movement's unorthodox structure. "We were marching not only against the destruction of the Emek theatre but also against discrimination toward LGBT+ individuals and against forces of

gentrification and precarious working conditions. We marched with queer activists, feminists, socialists and anarchists."

From the early-2000s to the mid-2010s, a flurry of directors made taboo-breaking films about Turkey's history. Yeşim Ustaoğlu's Journey to the Sun, Kazım Öz's The Photograph and Ahu Öztürk's Dust Cloth were part of what came to be known as "the new Turkish cinema". The oppressed voices of Turkish history, from Kurdish activists and labour organisers to human rights defenders and feminists, found a place in these films.

Yücel points to Dust Cloth, about two Kurdish cleaning women working in Istanbul's outskirts, which won prizes at Turkish festivals, as a particularly significant work. Seren Yüce's Majority, meanwhile, explored the ideological blindness of Turkish middle classes about the Kurdish question.

In those years, Yücel said, they could freely praise such films in the pages of Altyazı, whose offices were located on the Bosphorus University campus.

ABOVE: Erkan Yücel on the set of Anxiety, 1974

"Sometimes people would react to our references to the Kurdish massacres or the Armenian genocide, but that was about it."

Yet, a decade later, things have changed dramatically. Naci İnci, a rector appointed by Erdoğan, has taken over Bosphorus University, fired its top lecturers, including the documentary filmmaker Can Candan, closed down progressive student clubs, and destroyed the college's reputation as a home for Turkey's leading filmmakers. (Ceylan is an alumnus.)

Then Çiğdem Mater, the producer of Dust Cloth and Majority, was put behind bars. Mater has been in Bakırköy Prison in Istanbul since 25 April 2022. She and another filmmaker, Mine Özerden, were convicted of "attempting to topple the Turkish government" in 2013's Gezi protests and they were both sentenced to 18 years in prison.

The cases against Mater and Özerden began in 2015 when the government →

RIGHT: A still from the 2023 film *Kanun Hükmü* (The Decree). The film was banned from the Antalya Golden Orange Film Festival in Turkey

→ opened a case against the Taksim Solidarity, the initiative behind the Gezi events. The case expanded in 2017 when the philanthropist Osman Kavala was detained in an aeroplane at Istanbul's Atatürk Airport. He was later sentenced to life in prison.

Mater, meanwhile, was found guilty of "planning to make a film" about 2013's Gezi protests. In an interview with the Turkish press, she said her plans came to nothing due to financial reasons. But unbeknown to her, her phone was tapped and police were recording her discussions with potential funders for the film.

In her court case, Mater tried to prove that she had, in fact, never made a film about Gezi. The prosecutor proclaimed that it was only because the Gezi protests failed that Mater couldn't produce the film: the intention to produce the movie was sufficient for the 18-year prison sentence.

As of writing, five people remain in prison convicted of the Gezi case, and two are filmmakers.

"It's an absurd case," said Yücel. "If everyone who attended Gezi protests and filmed their experiences there joined forces, Mater could be released from prison." He thinks the government showed its savvy while designing the Gezi case. "By prosecuting people from various world views, they ensured there could be no unified resistance to the case. They fragmented the opposition successfully."

Another tactic employed by the government to further tar the name of Gezi activists took the form of propaganda films. In 2023, TRT,

Turkey's public broadcaster, released a limited series about Kavala titled Metamorphosis. Can Nergis plays the character of Teoman Bayramlı, a fictionalised avatar of the philanthropist. The film's script, penned by Mustafa Burak Doğu, portrays Kavala as an ex-communist who sold his soul to George Soros and other nefarious Western powers to stab the Turkish nation in the back.

Altyazı Fasikül described the TRT production as part of a smear campaign and scolded its attempt to "rewrite the personal history of Osman Kavala", who has been imprisoned for nearly seven years despite the European Court of Human Rights calling for his release.

As the captivity of two leading producers continues, new cases concerning the film community emerge by the day. In the week I spoke to Yücel, the filmmaker Koray Kesik was detained, arrested, charged with being a member of a terrorist organisation, and later released. Nejla Demirci's 2023 documentary *Kanun Hükmü* (The Decree), about a teacher and a doctor dismissed in the wake of the failed

2016 coup, was banned in Ankara and Istanbul and led to the cancellation of the Antalya Golden Orange Film Festival after its jury refused to stop its screening. That festival's jury president said he was threatened with death if they refused to cancel the screening.

Yücel said the film community should be more active and productive, "because this is how fear operates". He added: "If you give in to it once, your field of self-expression begins to shrink. You open this space for the government to limit you."

After the opposition's unprecedented electoral victory in March, there is hope. Yücel said he was cheered by the success of Hold Still at the Istanbul festival.

As for his practice, Yücel plans to continue interweaving filmmaking and film criticism. His films and writing will continue to search for the roots of Turkish autocracy in the country's history while refusing to disregard current affairs.

"We want to expand the scope of our films to the grassroots, the academia and beyond. We're using our networks to make sure our films reach wider audiences," he said. In that objective, Yücel is undoubtedly walking in his father's footsteps. ✘

*Kaya Genç is Index's contributing editor for Turkey*

53(02):74/78|DOI:10.1177/03064220241274940

## He was detained multiple times for these activities, yet he remained consistently unyielding

# Race, royalty and religion – Malaysian cinema's red lines

**DEBORAH AUGUSTIN** examines why the Kuala Lumpur government is censoring independent filmmakers

N 2020, DIRECTOR Khairi Anwar Jailani put out a call on social media for collaborators. He wanted to write and produce a film for a feature film competition. Khairi, who has a theatre background, got responses from two fellow theatre practitioners, co-writer and actor Arjun Thanaraju and producer Tan Meng Kheng.

With other collaborators, they wrote and eventually produced *Mentega Terbang* (2021). The film is about a young Malay Muslim girl who copes with her mother's terminal cancer diagnosis by exploring other religions, particularly what possible afterlives might exist outside of Islam, with the support of her parents. Outside of Malaysia, the film might seem innocuous. But in Muslim-majority Malaysia where apostasy laws exist for Muslims, the film breached touchy territory.

Yet despite the potentially sensitive themes of the movie, it received a warm reception at the small private screenings they organised in Malaysia and an overwhelmingly positive reception at an Indonesian film festival.

It was only in 2023 when the film debuted on the Hong Kong-based streaming platform Viu that things took a sinister turn. A Facebook post by conservative scriptwriter Zabidi Mohamed accused the film of blasphemy to Islam and his comments quickly went viral.

The harassment campaign led to a police investigation of the filmmakers,

the takedown of the film from Viu, and an attack on the cars of Thanaraju and Khairi. Meanwhile, Zabidi and the legion of social media commenters making threats were left unchecked. The film was banned in September 2023, months after the controversy died down. In response, Khairi and Tan filed a judicial review of the ban and after doing so found themselves charged under Section 298 of the Penal Code which refers to intentionally wounding the religious feelings of another.

Film censorship occupies a unique position in Malaysia. Film is the only medium of art where prior censorship exists, meaning that films undergo censorship prior to their release. Decisions made by the Film Censorship

Board (which falls under the Home Ministry) or LPF, its Malay language acronym, are final, under Section 48 of the Film Censorship Act 2002.

The draconian nature of film censorship in Malaysia dates back to British colonialism when the first censors were the police. Successive Malaysian governments have followed in the steps of their former colonisers in restricting criticisms of the status quo. Portraying the government, its agencies and the police in a negative or critical light is almost impossible. Under Prime Minister Anwar Ibrahim's current government it was hoped that some censorship might be eased but those hopes are dimming as the government tries to attract increasingly conservative  →

RIGHT: 2021 film *Mentega Terbang*, directed by Khairi Anwar Jailani

# If you show this film there might be repercussions

→ Malay-Muslim voters and avoid controversies that make it appear liberal or Western.

To skirt censorship guidelines and create more freely, independent filmmakers have up until now been in the habit of eschewing cinema releases, instead opting to go on the international festival circuit or a direct-to-streaming approach. Yet, the campaign by conservative critics to ban *Mentega Terbang*, and the charges against its creators are having a chilling effect on independent filmmakers.

For director Amanda Nell Eu, even international acclaim and an Oscar bid were not enough to shield her film from censorship. Eu's feature Tiger Stripes (2023), is a body-horror coming-of-age film about a young Muslim girl whose experience with puberty takes on a supernatural dimension. In 2023, Eu won the top prize at the Cannes' Critics Week, the first female Malaysian film maker to do so. Local media celebrated the film and Malaysia selected the film for Best International Feature Film at the

Oscars. However, a local theatrical run, a prerequisite for Oscar consideration, meant cuts. In a rare move for a local filmmaker, Eu made a statement speaking out about the censorship of her movie, stating she did not "stand behind the cut that will be shown in local cinemas." Eu has confessed in several interviews that she was scared of making such a statement. Eu elaborated on those fears: "You see how people can get really affected by storytelling. In Malaysia obviously, we see that happening to *Mentega Terbang*…and there's always backlash…That's very scary for the safety of filmmakers."

Eu believes it was the government desire to appeal to conservative voters which fueled some of the cuts her movie suffered. "When we were going through censorship, it was right after the Good Vibes Festival being cancelled," Eu said, referring to a music festival that was abruptly called off after the lead singer of British band The 1975 went on a rant about Malaysia's anti-LGBT+ laws and kissed bassist Ross MacDonald onstage. "So there's a lot of fear…If we allow this, what's going to happen? Is there going to be another big controversy? We don't want to deal with that."

Badrul Hisham Ismail, director of *Maryam Pagi ke Malam* (Maryam) (2023) found himself targeted by

conservatives in the shape of Zabidi, who was so instrumental in the banning of *Mentega Terbang*. The movie, Badrul's first feature film, is about a Muslim woman in her fifties navigating the Malaysian Sharia system so she can marry her younger fiancé from Sierra Leone. The protagonist Maryam is also a royal. Thus the movie touches on all three of the so-called 3Rs in Malaysia: race, religion and royalty. Essentially unofficial red lines.

The film was financed by a Covid-19 recovery grant for the arts from local government agency MyCreative Ventures. The grant did not require finished films to be screened locally. The only stipulation was that they needed to enter the film to at least one international film festival on a list of festivals provided by the agency.

CREDIT: (left) Richard Lim / Alamy; (right) Ghost Grrrl Pictures

......................................................

LEFT: 2023 film Tiger Stripes

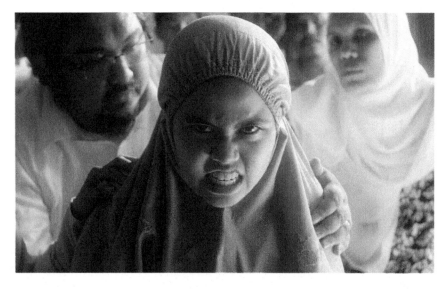

Initially, the filmmakers had no plans for local screenings but the reception by the Malaysian diaspora changed that. "We only decided to do [local screenings] because of the reaction that we got in [the International Film Festival] Rotterdam. How people were just telling us…try to share it with Malaysians however we can."

However after three private screenings, word about the movie got back to Zabidi. On 29 August 2023, Zabidi raised his objections to Maryam. He questioned why a movie made with government funds was not sent to LPF and screened locally. He also highlighted the fact that the movie would soon be screened at the Kota Bharu Film Festival in Kelantan, a conservative state ruled by the Islamist party Parti Islam Se-Malaysia (PAS). Badrul alerted the organisers of the film festival, "And then sure enough the next day, the organiser told me that the police came to them

and told them not to screen the film." Another planned screening of Maryam that was meant to fundraise for Sisters In Islam (SIS), a non-governmental organisation that advances Muslim women's rights, was also cancelled.

This happened despite the filmmakers' warnings to SIS to keep publicity for the screening discreet. "So they only share[d] within their network but somehow of course it got out also…And a week before the scheduled screening KDN went to the venue…and told DADI cinema that I heard you are showing this film next week. If you do, there might be repercussions."

For Badrul, the targeting of his film by Zabidi is indicative of the toxicity of the film industry at large that predates the current government: "I see Zabidi more as a symptom of how toxic and fragmented the industry is, rather than he is the cause of all this." He pointed out that the Film Act is from the colonial

ABOVE: Malaysian cinemas are no strangers to censorship

era, "We still use the pre-independent kind of Akta (Act)…[Film] was seen as a communication tool, it wasn't seen as art…and that sort of influenced how the industry's being governed."

Whatever the root cause of the increasing censorship, the banning of Mentega Terbang has cast a shadow over the independent filmmaking industry. For its co-writer Thanaraju, his prosecution has proved the last straw : "I don't feel like I can fully create films anymore. Because if I'm being perfectly honest, Mentega is the kind of film that I would make." ✖

*Deborah Augustin is Campaign and Strategy Lead at Freedom Film Network (FFN) in Malaysia*

53(02):79/81|DOI:10.1177/03064220241270334

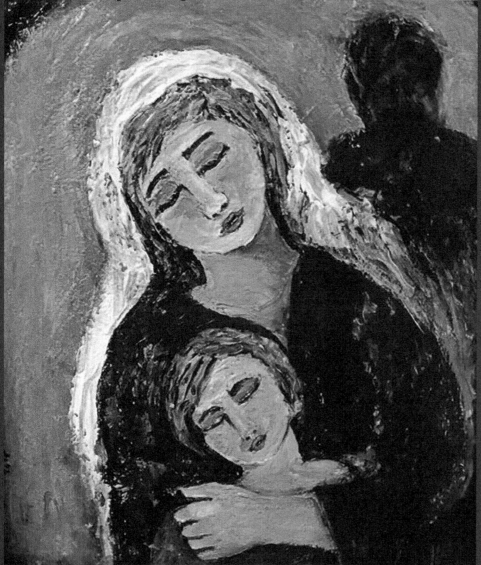

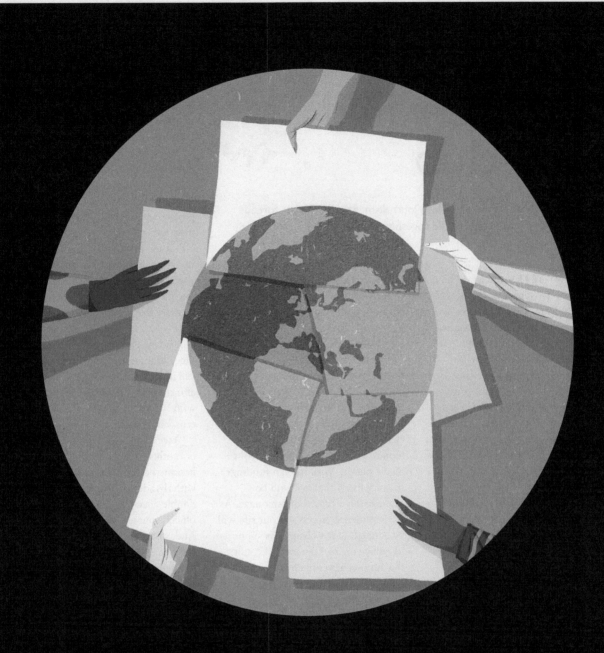

# COMMENT

"We must counter the threats from censorship
around the globe with solidarity on a global scale"

JOIN THE EXILED PRESS CLUB | CAN DÜNDAR | P.84

# Join the exiled press club

CAN DÜNDAR, a titan of Turkish journalism, says journalists forced to work overseas need to band together to take on the tyrants

IN RECENT YEARS, the world has witnessed the spread of a new type of journalism: journalism in exile. On the one hand, repressive regimes have become more widespread. On the other hand, technological capabilities have increased. This has led to a rise in the number of journalists working outside their home countries, and many media outlets have since begun to reach their audiences across borders. Mine is one of those.

After a news report I made in Turkey on the transfer of Turkish weapons to Syrian fighters was deemed a "state secret", I was sentenced to 28 years in prison and was the target of an assassination attempt. I was compelled to continue my profession outside the country.

The last seven years of my 45 as a journalist have been spent in Berlin. As soon as I arrived in the city, I established a media platform called Özgürüz ("We are free"). After dissident journalists from Turkey joined, Afghan colleagues came, then Ukrainians and Russians, and now Palestinians.

Wherever there is oppression or war in the world, journalists who are excluded from their home countries and are scattered around

the globe are trying to overcome the wall of censorship and reach people back home through their work. This growing trend has become an important contribution to the struggle for truth. However, being far away from oppressive environments does not mean that the problems are over – quite the contrary, as I have learnt.

Here are just some of the challenges. First and foremost, money. How will you finance your media outlet? With foreign funding? It's very likely that you will be immediately accused of espionage. As a consequence, access to your site will be banned. Our website was supposed to go live on 24 January 2017, but the Turkish government's ban was issued on 23 January without it even knowing the content (something condemned by Index and 38 other civil organisations at the time). Thus, we gained the honour of being the first website shut down before its launch. The political-military-economic relations of the country you are broadcasting from with the country you come from are important, too. The country you're broadcasting from is not always prepared to risk profitable trade for free media.

Can you instead finance your media outlet through subscriptions?

Would people send contributions if that meant taking the risk of being branded as "terrorism supporters"?

Then there is the question of operations. What about staff?

Yes, our numbers are growing – but it is still hard finding media professionals in exile. Contributing from within is extremely risky. What if they use pen names? Would their correspondence be monitored? What about you, yourself? Even if free in your new land, you are under pressure to start and finance a new life, learn a new language and overcome bureaucratic restrictions. At the same time, your family, your loved ones, are still in the country you left. Can you afford to risk their lives with what you write? With this very question, self-censorship begins to replace censorship.

Access to resources and to sources is another problem. Most will hesitate before sharing information with dissidents. The possibility of double-checking information from official sources is almost non-existent. And, of course, there is the security problem. In our case, Turkish intelligence wasted little time before identifying our address and sending a pro-government TV channel crew to "raid" us. One day, out of the blue, a crew broadcast outside our door – "The den of treason!"

They showed the building, down to the window of our office, gave the address and announced our arrival and departure times. From then on, we were open targets.

Let's say you overcome all this. How would you reach your audience?

We've been playing Whac-A-Mole with the government ever since we first went on air. We have tried to give a voice through every communication channel possible: YouTube, Periscope, Facebook, Twitter, Instagram. If one got blocked, we'd air through another. The address of the site we are currently publishing on is **ozguruz7.org**. Why "7"? Because the

> ## Each time they blocked us, we added a new number after our name and went back on air

CREDIT: (portrait) Milena Schloesser; (illustration) Emma Hanquist / Ikon Images

first six were blocked. Each time they blocked us, we added a new number after our name and went back on air the next day.

Another example in the field of book publishing shows a censorship workaround. Despite being published in seven languages, my book's Turkish edition was banned in Turkey. In the end, we offered readers there the opportunity to download the book for free. We reached 30,000 readers within a week.

Then there is Forbidden Stories, a

# Just as autocrats who censor us mimic and learn from each other, we must collaborate with each other

project in which journalists pick up stories where others were forced to leave, and RSF's pioneering initiative to launch the Svoboda Satellite Package that provides independent journalism to Russian-speaking populations.

Both are important initiatives that

show how journalists in exile can thwart censorship back home. We've had too many troubles to count; yet, as these examples show, it is possible to insist on telling the truth. Nay, it is essential. The first rule is to never give up. This resolve means you'll find ways to overcome all the above troubles, since courage is no less infectious than fear.

And we must now globalise this courage. We must counter the threats from censorship around the globe with solidarity on a global scale. Just as autocrats who censor us mimic and learn from each other, we must collaborate with each other.

Here is my proposal: There is an urgent need for an organisation that brings together exiled journalists striving to pursue the truth in different corners of the world under one umbrella. Such an organisation would facilitate easy exchange of information, enable members to benefit from each other's experiences, give them the opportunity to exchange ideas for new journalistic standards appropriate to the new conditions, and serve as a primary news source for the media in the countries they are based. We'd discuss all the above problems and also all the above solutions.

International solidarity and the courage that transcends borders makes it easier to overcome censorship of truth, wherever we may be. Together we can form the most powerful alliance of exiled journalists. So, who's joining me? ✖

*Can Dündar is an award-winning Turkish journalist, filmmaker and author*

53(02):84/85|DOI:10.1177/03064220241274941

# Freedoms lost in translation

LEFT: Bänoo Zan speaks at Shab-e She'r, the poetry night she founded in Canada in 2012

Poet **BÄNOO ZAN** describes how censorship works for refugee and immigrant writers in Canada

CENSORSHIP IN LITERATURE can be implemented with the best of intentions, or in the name of highest values.

But in dictatorships and totalitarian regimes, there is state censorship in the name of national security or cultural and religious identity. And, of course, almost everything worth saying is targeted by the censors. Even writings that are not censored lose their significance in the absence of counter arguments and diverse viewpoints. Censorship in such countries is maintained by force, threats, intimidation, jail sentences, assassinations and other coercive methods.

I was born and raised in such a place: Iran. I studied and taught English literature at Iranian universities, and in 2010 I emigrated to Canada and started to explore the English language literary scene. I joined workshops and attended readings, book launches and open mics.

I published a book in Iran and here in Canada, and I published two more, sat on juries and editorial panels, ran workshops and published more than 300 poems, essays, and translations in magazines around the globe.

In 2012, I founded Shab-e She'r (Poetry Night), a monthly poetry reading and open mic series based on values of diversity and freedom of speech. These reflections of my experience of Western censorship are based on my encounters with poets, writers, members of literary juries, editors, publishers and organisers in the Canadian and immigrant literary scenes, as well as my observation of patterns of acceptance and rejection of my own writing by English language literary magazines and book publishers based in the USA, the UK, Canada and Europe.

The book I published in Iran was submitted to the state censor in the Ministry of Culture and Islamic Guidance. In Western democracies, censorship is usually in the form of peer and self-censorship. This is maintained in the name of freedom of speech or diversity. It stems from the fear of being dominated by minorities, the fear of backlash by hardliners, or the fear of being unkind to minorities. It operates mainly through manuscript rejections by publishers and editors, retraction of articles, loss of opportunities and disinvitations.

Poets and writers who leave their repressive homelands for the West may at first think that they have escaped censorship. Those who continue to write in their mother tongues may never know otherwise. In Canada, many immigrant and refugee writers keep writing in their native language. And since the censorship office in the Islamic Republic of Iran does not have jurisdiction in Canada, Iranian writers in exile can "freely" express themselves in Persian. The problem, however, is that since they are writing in a language unknown to most Canadians, the mainstream Canadian reading and writing community cannot access their writing.

Exiled writers are separated from their linguistic community. For instance, the majority of Persian language publishers and readers are in Iran, Tajikistan and Afghanistan. Separation from the speakers of the language makes it difficult for the writer to keep in touch with changing nuances in language and culture. Loss of readership and community limit the writers' impact as well. Living in ethnic neighborhoods in the West may partially solve the issue, but it disconnects exiled writers from the mainstream arts and culture scene of their adopted countries.

As a result, writers in exile are censored out of their native and host literary scenes: censorship through marginalisation. It is only when immigrants write in the official languages of their adopted countries that they begin to perceive limitations on freedom of speech.

The censorship controversies that get into the news mark a later stage in the process. For censorship to be newsworthy, the author must already be published or have secured a high-profile speaking gig. But censorship starts much earlier than that. Because of the competitive nature of publishing and the lack of forgiveness towards those deemed ideologically erratic, self-censorship is the practice of many writers. This habit is detrimental to their intellectual clarity and honesty, turning writing into a negotiation with the powers of untruth.

If a writer manages to overcome

## Writers in exile are censored out of their native and host literary scenes

self-censorship and produce a text that is original and authentic, the next stage is to secure a publishing deal. This is the most daunting stage. In democracies, writers' peers are their most formidable censors. And

what these peers are influenced by matters a lot.

The literary scene is split roughly into two camps. One camp supports freedom of speech. The progressives in this camp believe

in global solidarity among social justice causes. They support political writers who raise awareness about human rights abuses in their home countries. Many literary circles in this camp were formed by those  →

# Very few literary outlets encourage writers to be truth-tellers

→ who experienced the 1960s and 1970s and are leftists or liberals in the older sense of the words. They are anti-dictatorial as much as they are anti-colonial. They believe in universal values that connect diverse struggles for social justice around the world. This camp may not be as ethnically diverse, but it believes that freedom of speech allows individuals to combat inequality.

This camp no longer sets the tone of debate on the left, nor does it control the narrative in the mainstream literary scene. It is sidelined by a newer left that is more interested in issues of identity. One other factor that detracts from the influence that this camp can have is the emergence of online platforms and publications that are controlled by the younger generation who mostly subscribe to the values of the newer left.

Others who belong to the free speech camp have other agendas and lean to the political right. They betray an antagonistic attitude towards specific countries, regions and religions. They welcome self-critical minority writers, but not minority writers critical of the West. Joining the right-wing camp may at times feel like betraying your roots. Hence, some immigrants, refugees and people of colour may not feel they belong.

At the opposite end of the spectrum, there is a camp that promotes diversity – a laudable cause. But the way it proposes to achieve this end is through limiting speech. In its efforts to achieve equity and inclusivity, it resorts to tactics such as refusal to publish, deplatforming, retracting writing from (online) magazines, and pressuring organisations and employers to fire or disinvite writers, thinkers and activists.

Its goal is to delegitimise certain ideas by marginalising them. It is the newer left: more anti-colonial than anti-dictatorial. In fact, it is curiously silent about dictators who hold their own populations hostage in the name of religion, nationality or identity.

This camp is indifferent to human rights abuses beyond Western borders. International issues are dismissed until they become Western issues, such as the current Israel-Palestine conflict. What is happening in Sudan, Afghanistan or other regions is irrelevant to this camp. It denounces as racist those who disagree with the terms and definitions it holds sacrosanct. This camp is mainly interested in positive and uplifting stories that glorify religions, countries, cultures and ethnicities from the global south. This is the group that has the most power and influence and today controls the narrative in the publishing world.

It should be noted that in the current artistic and political climate, even publishers who say they believe in freedom of expression will not publish work that may bring the ire of diversity advocates and Islamists upon their head. When they do, they quickly remove the controversial piece. The same fate awaits speaking gigs and featured readings.

Many writers are critical of their own – especially refugee and immigrant writers who have left their homelands because of political, social, cultural and artistic suppression. Although the newer left may validate some components of these writers' identity, it coerces them into silence and conformity and discourages them from adopting a self-critical outlook. As a result, the newer left in the publishing industry here in

Canada ends up promoting mainly North American writers born and raised in Canada or assimilated into the Canadian culture. Immigrant and refugee writers who have experienced life under dictatorships and corrupt regimes find that they do not quite belong to this camp.

Minoritised writers, therefore, find themselves in a dilemma: one camp wants them to criticise only their own culture while the other demands that they only praise it. Very few literary outlets encourage writers to be truth-tellers.

Many immigrant or refugee writers don't find it worth their while to write in a foreign language only to play into the hands of those who reduce them to propagandists for or against their culture.

In Toronto, there are innumerable reading series and poetry events but, as far as I know, Shab-e She'r is the only regular poetry event founded and run by an immigrant. Hence, it falls into neither camp. I tell the audiences that the answer to a poem is another poem – not a call to silence the offending voice. Diverse means diverse from you, whoever you are and however you identify.

Adrienne Rich famously rejected the National Medal of the Arts in 1997 to protest inequality in the USA under president Bill Clinton, saying: "Art – in my own case the art of poetry – means nothing if it simply decorates the dinner table of power which holds it hostage."

Freedom and art are inseparable. As the writing community, we need to examine the powers that hold us hostage. ✖

*Bänoo Zan is a poet and the founder and organiser of Shab-e She'r in Toronto, and co-editor of Woman, Life, Freedom: Poems for the Iranian Revolution, published in 2024*

53(02):86/88|DOI:10.1177/03064220241274942

'Exhilarating . . . skilfully dramatises the extraordinary chain of events that led to the end of Soviet power'

*Observer*

'Fascinating and revelatory . . . engrossing and dramatic . . . adds a new, captivating chapter to the history of the Cold War'

*New Statesman*

'An intensely moving story that explores the nature of freedom'

*Sunday Times*

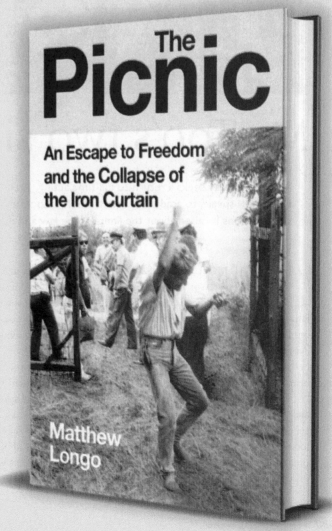

The **Picnic**

An Escape to Freedom and the Collapse of the Iron Curtain

Matthew Longo

VINTAGE

# Me Too's two sides

ABOVE: The #MeToo movement sparked global protests against sexual violence, including this march in San Francisco

As Kevin Spacey seeks a return to full-time acting, **JOHN SCOTT LEWINSKI** speaks to academics about the #MeToo movement and the questions it raised about the limits of the law and due process

LAURA BETH NIELSEN, a USA-based law professor focusing on the law's ability to change, laments the lack of nuanced thinking on display in the wake of #MeToo. People have struggled to navigate believing accusers while remaining open-minded for the accused.

"These issues require us to be smart and thoughtful, not just polarised, vengeful or defensive," Nielsen told Index. "I don't know if we have that capacity in this society now. These offences differ. Bill Cosby is on a

completely different level from someone who accidentally misgenders someone – or someone who is wrongfully accused for any variety of reasons."

Nielson's concerns were raised by people such as author Margaret Atwood at the time, who said the #MeToo movement was the symptom of a broken legal system and had been "seen as a massive wake-up call". But she also asked: "If the legal system is bypassed because it is seen as ineffectual, what will take its place? Who will be the new power brokers?"

The emergence of the #MeToo movement in 2017 put serial predators and sexual harassers on notice. Their crimes would no longer go unchecked or be dismissed with a wink and a nod by a culture more concerned with fame and fortune than the suffering of women or the vulnerable.

The accused abusers identified by #MeToo roughly fell into a few categories of offences and punishment. In the cases of Harvey Weinstein, Jeffrey Epstein, Danny Masterson and Bill Cosby, the justice system acted with systematic finality, ending the careers of all concerned and imprisoning all but Cosby (who regained his freedom only due to a technical prosecutorial error). Those men will be known as rapists or

CREDIT: Sundry Photography / Alamy

traffickers for the rest of their lives – and beyond as Epstein's legacy proves.

Others, including Dustin Hoffman, Louis CK and Kevin Spacey, faced a public reckoning even if they were never formally found guilty (in Spacey's case a UK criminal court found him not guilty while a new documentary, Spacey Unmasked, detailed separate allegations). Some alleged abusers admitted wrongdoing and asked for forgiveness with varying degrees of contriteness. Occasionally, they claimed the sexual encounters never occurred or were consensual.

Finally, there were those individuals accused of abuse or other unacceptable behaviour online or via the media. They were not charged officially and there may be no evidence beyond accusations.

Nielsen says the brand of potential censorship involved in #MeToo cases is social and not official or state-sponsored, making it more difficult to identify or prevent. As for alleged predators being "cancelled" – losing their public reputations or ability to make a living in their chosen fields – she makes it clear they have limited recourse, even if they seek legal responses such as libel, slander or defamation claims.

Nielsen looks to legal procedures to aid her personal evaluation of alleged sexual misconduct.

"Once someone is convicted or held liable, I'm not going to buy their product," she explained. "That's a decision as a consumer. I'm not concerned with their claims that 'I've been cancelled, and I can't work anymore'. Yes, if you've been rightly found guilty or responsible, people will make their decisions as they've done before with other issues and actions.

"They have a right to make a living. But they don't have a right to make a living however they wish. When it comes to something like the entertainment industry, audiences can vote with their wallets."

But she worries about a brand of rushed mob justice in the court of public opinion, and sees little informed guidance from cultural leadership to help navigate that.

"As with so many other issues today, everybody becomes stridently oppositional – from extreme feminists to men's rights activists," she said. "If it becomes 'Only believe women! Only believe men!' we're not going to get to a starting point in a more fair or neutral place to explore what is proven and what we can believe."

Deborah Tuerkheimer, a professor at the Northwestern University Pritzker School of Law, published a study, Unofficial Reporting in the #MeToo Era, in the University of Chicago Legal Forum. It states: "#MeToo is sparking the creation of new channels for reporting abuse – channels intended to bypass the laws and rules that prohibit sexual misconduct."

Just as #MeToo perpetrators can be broken down into the unofficial classifications above, Tuerkheimer disperses the reporting of sexual abuse and exploitation into her own categories: the Traditional Whisper Network, the Double Secret Whisper Network, the Shadow Court of Public Opinion and the New Court of Public Opinion. The Traditional Whisper Network spreads victim experiences and accusations of abuse via in-person or one-to-one communications to protect the anonymity of the abuse reporter. The Double Secret Whisper Network spreads similar information via social media and other technology, reaching a larger community much faster while still protecting the privacy of the accuser. The Shadow Court of Opinion uses widespread open online forums and social media to share anonymous accounts of sexual misconduct.

"Notwithstanding the controversial nature of these platforms and questions of legal liability that surround them, for accusers intent on

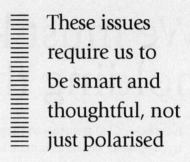

## These issues require us to be smart and thoughtful, not just polarised

publicly exposing their abuser without identifying themselves, the Shadow Court of Public Opinion beckons," Tuerkheimer said. Finally, the New Court of Public Opinion abandons degrees of anonymity to allow openly public stories of abuse and identification of attackers.

While these four stages finally exposed the monstrous, seemingly endless crimes of the likes of Weinstein, Masterson and Epstein, they also threatened to brand other alleged perpetrators without giving them the opportunity to defend their presumed innocence.

All four of Tuerkheimer's groupings beg a simple question: Is it possible to engage in a culture that exposes abuse and supports accusers, acknowledges the problems of evidence around crimes of a sexual nature and also acknowledges degrees of offence and the concept of reasonable doubt?

As Western culture continues the complex struggle of balancing support for victims while presuming the innocence of the accused, the #MeToo movement has developed into the most human of institutions. Made necessary by cruelty, created for justice, intended for compassion and fuelled by rage, that simple hashtag retains the power to expose abuse but also to marginalise the incorrectly targeted. ✖

*John Scott Lewinski is a freelance journalist based in the USA*

53(02):90/91|DOI:10.1177/03064220241274943

# We must keep holding the line

New Index CEO **JEMIMAH STEINFELD** explains why standing up for dissidents is more important than ever

AS REMARKABLE AS this might sound for someone who's been connected to Index on Censorship for almost a decade, I've never been trolled. Until this May, that is.

My undoing? A post on X about Tiananmen Square.

I knew this could invite criticism from China's Little Pinks, the army of young, jingoistic nationalists who prowl the online world waiting to jump on anyone or anything anti-Chinese Communist Party (CCP).

What I didn't expect was anti-Semitic trolling. All the cliched slurs were rolled out and among them was a recurring one – I wasn't allowed an opinion because I was Jewish (which they must have assumed based on my surname) and therefore, by extension, part of a state committing genocide.

Apparently, because of the actions of Israel – a country I am not from – I'd lost my moral authority and right to a voice. I was essentially told to shut up.

To reiterate: I've never been trolled before. To reiterate: this was a post about China.

Now there's every chance that my detractors came from fake accounts related to the CCP rather than real accounts. But they were clearly amplifying current divisions within our societies.

Welcome to the world of free expression. We talk about how free speech has been captured by angry, middle-aged white men to justify right-wing views. But what of those people who claim to care about human rights – about Palestinian lives in particular – who are attacking others simply for being Jewish?

Such voices do not represent the mainstream, fortunately (contrary to what our governments – who already want to clamp down on protest rights – would have us believe). They're just a lot more prolific these days.

I start my first column as CEO of Index not to say "woe is me". I am incredibly lucky.

I won't be arrested for it – unlike, say, the Iranian rapper Toomaj Salehi, who until very recently has been sitting on death row simply for singing about human rights. Unlike Sophia Huang Xueqin, who is in jail in China for feminist activism. Unlike Vladimir Kara-Murza, a British-Russian journalist who spoke out against the war in Ukraine and is behind bars.

These people are reminders that what we face in the UK is nothing compared to what others face.

The trolling was also more mesmerising than upsetting. If I had to do a vodka shot every time someone called me a CIA stooge, I'd still be drunk.

It was very much a case of sticks and stones – nothing actually hurt.

Still, to paraphrase the late, great Stephen Spender in Index's founding statement, even if such an example might not have led to injury, it nonetheless matters. Democracies don't die in the dark. They die in the open when enough people either don't care, or look the other way, or allow their movements to be hijacked by bad actors – be that governments which already want to clamp down on free speech, or those which want to attach themselves to a noble cause, or both.

Just look at Hungary. There, an unending drumbeat of propaganda has demonised minority groups. There, Viktor Orbán (who once sat on the left) has hidden behind the pretence that the existence of opposition parties (who don't get a fair hearing) and civil society (which is stymied by endless regulation) makes Hungary less of a dictatorship.

As the old Yiddish proverb goes, a half-truth is really a whole lie, but this lie has been little challenged by policy makers and, as loathed as he is by many, others within Hungary support him.

Since 7 October 2023, majoritarianism has become far more widespread, reaching places that are upheld as democracies. This form of majoritarianism says if you're not fully with us you're against us, that identity matters above all else, and that we can be divided neatly into camps.

It is taking some of those who should be allies in the fight against authoritarianism with it and it's emboldening those who already harbour bigoted opinions.

It didn't magically appear last October. Years of "cancelling" people, of identity politics first, of talking about "the right side of history" (as if the past were so easily divided into good and bad, rather than messy and morally compromised) set the stage. It was facilitated by social media, the platforms becoming powerhouses for

## Some are even scared to ask a question for fear it's the 'wrong sort'

smearing, facilitated by governments and leaders across the world – and we fell for it.

Free speech has become unfashionable – a bit like feminism when I was growing up, which many wrongly assumed meant you hated men. Today if you say the words "free speech" there's a knee-jerk assumption that it's just for those who want carte blanche to hate minorities. But like feminism, at its core, free speech is about equality – an equality of voice. Does that mean free speech is always nice? No. As George Orwell said, for it to work, sometimes you get told what you don't want to hear.

But it's the oxygen of social justice. Without it we can't call out anything.

Does that mean free speech is always easy? Alas, no. We don't always agree on when sincere political speech becomes hate speech. We don't always agree on what to do about hate speech, either. Should we shut it down straight away? Should we create a sub-category – "harmful speech" – and intervene only once it lands there? What is harm and who gets to define it? None of these has an obvious answer. But a failure to confidently judge here does

not automatically mean a moral failure on the part of the person adjudicating.

Fuelled in part by these challenges we've retreated. Self-censorship has crept in. Some are even scared to ask a question for fear it's the "wrong sort". It's suffocating.

The real winners are the tyrants. China's Xi Jinping. Russia's Vladimir Putin. Iran's Ayatollah Ali Khamenei. They look to countries such as the USA and the UK and laugh when we fall short. "What a mess democracy is," Chinese state media said when the UK was tearing itself apart in the weeks following the Brexit vote.

We really need to hold the line on free speech right now – in principle and in practice. More people are living under "partly free" or "not free" regimes compared with open ones, according to a Freedom House report released earlier this year.

India tilted the scales. Prime minister Narendra Modi was dealt a blow in June – and yet he is still in power. Will he be a diminished statesman entering his last term or will he be vengeful and further erode India's rights landscape?

Elsewhere, the catalogue of concern

ABOVE: Protesters from the Democratic Party of China march to the Chinese Consulate General in New York to commemorate the Tiananmen Square Massacre on its 35th anniversary

is too long to list, so just consider this: France – the country of *liberté, égalité, fraternité* – has called a snap election to stave off the far right; even before the current war, Israel under Benjamin Netanyahu was struggling to lay claim to the title of the Middle East's only democracy; and in the USA, another Donald Trump term is looming and he's already said he'll go after his critics in the harshest way. So much for First Amendment rights.

Index was created on the back of calls for help from dissidents in the Soviet Union during the Cold War. We were always about dissidents, and we shall remain so. The problem is that if we continue to narrow the parameters of acceptable speech over here, we'll become dissidents, too, and that won't be for noble reasons.

Then who will hold the line? ✖

*Jemimah Steinfeld is Index CEO*

53(02):92/93|DOI:10.1177/03064220241274944

# WOMAN LIFE FREEDOM

## Voices and Art from the Women's Protests in Iran

**SAQI**

www.saqibooks.com

18-24 Turnham Green Terrace,
London W4 1QP

T:(020) 7221 9347

A DEEPLY MOVING TESTIMONY TO RESISTANCE, THIS UNIQUE COLLECTION IS THE FIRST TO SHOWCASE ART AND WRITING FROM THE WOMEN'S PROTESTS IN IRAN.

Jina Mahsa Amini's death at the hands of Iran's Morality Police on 16 September 2022 sparked widespread protests across the country. Women took to the streets, uncovering their hair, burning headscarves and chanting 'Woman Life Freedom' – 'Zan Zendegi Azadi' in Persian and 'Jin Jîyan Azadî' in Kurdish – in mass demonstrations. An explosion of creative resistance followed as art and photography shared online went viral and people around the world saw what was really going on in Iran.

*Woman Life Freedom* captures this historic moment in artwork and first-person accounts. Extolling the power of art, writing and body politics – both female and queer – this collection is a universal rallying call and a celebration of the women the regime has tried and failed to silence.

£14.99 ◆ Non-Fiction ◆ Paperback ◆ eBook available

The Smarties, Tehran, photo © Shiva Khademi

# CULTURE

"In this story of the Palestinian people there
was something sick. From 1948 to today, love
and life have progressively disappeared"

THE UNSTILLED VOICE OF GAZAN THEATRE | LAURA SILVIA BATTAGLIA | P.104

# It's not Normal

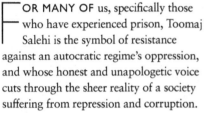

**NAZANIN ZAGHARI-RATCLIFFE** introduces a song by rapper **TOOMAJ SALEHI** whose death sentence has been reversed but who still languishes in an Iranian jail

LEFT: Nazanin Zaghari-Ratcliffe speaking at a conference in 2023

FOR MANY OF us, specifically those who have experienced prison, Toomaj Salehi is the symbol of resistance against an autocratic regime's oppression, and whose honest and unapologetic voice cuts through the sheer reality of a society suffering from repression and corruption.

To us, condemning Salehi to death for his songs and lyrics is the equivalent of declaring war against the people of Iran.

The first time I heard Salehi was right at the beginning of the Woman, Life, Freedom movement. He seemed like an ordinary man with a real voice in his music, suddenly thrown into the national and international spotlight while holding onto his truth. His music showed the power of ordinary voices in Iran and beyond.

Salehi has long challenged the Islamic Republic of Iran's establishment. Through his songs and lyrics, he has condemned the state's political repression, injustice, corruption and violation of women's rights for many years. As a result, he has gained fans amongst Iranians inside and outside the country while managing to outrage the government.

Salehi condemns the Islamic state for its corruption, which increases the gap in society where the poor get poorer and the rich become richer. In his song Normal, he speaks bluntly about a rampant poverty which is inflicted on a resource-rich country. Salehi articulates how sanctions, as well as self-inflicted international isolation, have resulted in a huge part of society hardly being able to make ends meet while those in power are busy building tower blocks and pocketing wealth at home and abroad.

Salehi tells of his ambitions for living in a normal country, where people can have the freedom to speak and criticise their political leaders and to defend their basic rights without being harassed, prosecuted or imprisoned.

At the heat of the Woman, Life, Freedom movement in Iran in September 2022, following the death of Mahsa Amini while in the custody of the morality police, Salehi released several songs in support of the movement, which increased his popularity amongst the people but also the anger of the authorities. He was arrested, and he was released on bail only after the Supreme Court overturned the charges in November 2023.

The state has systematically used forced confession to silence and repress dissent for decades and on his release, Salehi posted a YouTube video in which he described the torture and forced confession he went through while in detention. Three days later, the security forces raided his house in Isfahan and arrested him again. Salehi was sentenced to death by the Revolutionary Court of Isfahan in April 2024.

After an Index-led campaign the Supreme Court ruled out the death penalty but Salehi remains at the time of publication behind bars. Like many others, he finds himself trapped in this circle of corruption and power. Freedom for Salehi is a world where he is allowed to articulate his vision without being punished; in which the government is willing to improve people's daily lives, and a regime which does not indoctrinate its citizens and ensures they have the means to live dignified lives.

Through his music, he tries to be the voice of those terrified to speak up, and it is only fair to echo his voice beyond his country's borders.

*Nazanin Zaghari-Ratcliffe is a former hostage in Iran and author of the forthcoming book A Yard of Sky: A Story of Love, Resistance and Hope*

## Normal

| By Toomaj Salehi

Yes! Yes Sir! Life is normal
A labourer's annual wage is worth a dinner abroad

Yes! Of course, Sir! Life is normal
We don't dare say otherwise, lest we get in trouble
Yes! Yes Sir! Life is normal
Some have to sleep in tombs, others own 10 high-rises
Yes! Of course, Sir! Life is normal
We don't ask for what is ours, lest it be a crime

Sir, have you seen down there? The empty plates?
You are so enlightened, have you seen the dark city?
Have you seen these quarters where the waists are so narrowed, from your blood-sucking
These quarters where you dump your waste from above
Have you seen how different we are?
Be my guest, no need to buy tickets to watch
Kid! Go back back to your room, you are scaring the gentleman
He is not used to seeing ragged and worn clothes, not even from afar
Are you watching Sir?
You shine like a star, with the glimmering light of the ones you executed
Instead of being reprimanded, you have been promoted for your mistakes
You cut off any dissident at will
Sir! My words are sour, have some sweets to wash off the taste
Here, people are just alive, they don't have a life
Our kids sleep with empty stomachs
Sorry, how do you sleep with a clear conscience again?

Yes! Yes Sir! Life is normal
A labourer's annual wage is worth a dinner abroad
Yes! Of course, Sir! Life is normal
We don't dare say otherwise, lest we get in trouble
Yes! Yes Sir! Life is normal
Some have to sleep in tombs, others own 10 high-rises
Yes! Of course, Sir! Life is normal
We don't ask for what is ours, lest it be a crime

While the rest of the world is supporting their citizens
Our government denied responsibility and kept complaining
It called protesters insurrectionists
Did it stop at imprisonment? No, it committed atrocities (as well)
No doubt "We broke records"!
We are the only country, where the (COVID) vaccine was different for the rich and poor
In the age of science, women are beaten for their beauty,
Thrown in the back of a police van, taken to unnamed prisons
Our shopping cart is empty, no more oil left to export
The rest of the world are shooting for the moon and mars, while we are in the abyss
We are the dead who can't die
Since we can't pay for the burial and the tombstone
 I'm ringing the alarms, hoping ears burn
We have people who are on the verge of death from starvation

→

→ They have kissed the lips of death, where are they?
Perhaps someone should sing them lullabies
Yes! Yes Sir! Life is normal
A labourer's annual wage is worth a dinner abroad
Yes! Of course, Sir! Life is normal
We don't dare say otherwise, lest we get in trouble
Yes! Yes Sir! Life is normal
Some have to sleep in tombs, others own 10 high-rises
Yes! Yes Sir! Life is normal
We don't ask for what is ours, lest it be a crime

We are constantly worried about the rent
We are scared for roofless schools in the desert
A bird can't fly without food and water
Is this a normal life, or are we sick?
Cheap products cost a fortune
Labourer is working overtime, yet the car he wants to buy is getting further away
In this corrupt cycle, he is struggling
The regime sacrifices a million for one
For the deeply corrupt regime apologists in the US
Those who compensate for their inferiority by debauchery
There is no Left and Right here, they are all the same
We say we are trapped in a swamp, they say they hope to reform it
Is there anything that makes you feel ashamed?
Do you think citizens are your slaves?
You expect people not to eat bread so yours is buttered?
Did I confuse you by calling you Sir?

Oil tankers in a queue, on their way
Red tulip covered lands, green dollar bills
The poverty ridden city, the only sound is the cry of death
To hell with the regime officials
We are all united, We want freedom
Locked hands, human chains
We are all united, We want freedom
The power of unity is ours
Oil tankers in a queue, on their way
Red tulip covered lands, green dollar bills
The poverty ridden city, the only sound is the cry of death
To hell with the regime officials ✖

*Toomaj Salehi is an Iranian rapper who received an Index Freedom of Expression Award in 2023. A year later after he was sentenced to death in Iran Index launched a petition signed by leading cultural figures calling for his death sentence to be immediately and unconditionally quashed and for him to be released from detention, with all other charges dismissed. At the time of publication the Supreme Court has reversed his death sentence, but he is still behind bars. Lyrics translated by TurfHeadClic on Lyricstranslate.com*

53(02):96/98|DOI:10.1177/0306422024I27I525

# No offence intended

Imagine making a film so sensitive that no one in the world could possibly be upset. Wouldn't it be the most popular movie ever made?

## Headhunted

### By Kaya Genç

IN 2023, SOON after we resettled in California, my phone started ringing. It was our first week at the quaint green-leafed house at the end of a winding path. The college had provided this lofty refuge to our use, and we couldn't be happier living in a home surrounded by towering trees and located in California, one of the most expensive places to live in the world. I had come here to write a novel and didn't think much about employment or work; I'd emotionally support my wife, who taught at a liberal college and lay low for a while. So imagine my surprise when the voice at the end of the phone, with its whispery tone, said she wanted to headhunt me.

The woman was perhaps younger than me (I'm 43) and said she worked for the "biggest streaming service in the world". They recently had issues with "sensitivities and censorship" and were facing "headwinds" from all directions. Autocratic and democratic countries around the globe were demanding "more sensitivity, even censorship" from their "content". Coming from Turkey (characterised by me as "a relentless censorship regime" in a year-old article she quoted), I could be an ideal sensitivity reader for the company. Their headquarters were located nearby, in Los Gatos, California. Would I be game?

"A sensitivity reader?" my wife laughed, pouring espresso into adjacent porcelain cups. "And whose sensitivities would you be monitoring?"

"Not a clue," I said, gulping down the bitter coffee, which tasted so good despite its ordinary Trader Joe's brand. "It's funny I'm being headhunted here of all places. Nobody offered me a job back in Istanbul. Now we're out in the wild, and look what happens."

I had a risqué reputation in Turkey. My friends jokingly recommended I readied a packed bag by the door like Soviet dissidents, as I could soon be "taken away" for some made-up charge after my two decades of rattling government feathers. I jokingly disbelieved them.

\* \* \*

On Monday afternoon, my wife drove me to Los Gatos. She dropped me at the door of the company headquarters like a mailed-back DVD boxset full of scratches. The building resembled a palace—and bore an eerie likeness to the gilded Palace of our esteemed Turkish hegemon.

The headhuntress picked me up at the lobby. She was petite, her blonde hair pony-tailed, and her garments (black Issey Miyake turtleneck, plain blue jeans) were Valleyesque. She offered to show me around.

There were "live-edge" dining tables in the cafeteria. We walked past a wall-less conference room sitting atop a circular red carpet. We passed by theatres where producers beta-tested their "content". The company's iconic red colour dominated the halls. There were red leather chairs, red doors and red lighting equipment, and soon, we were walking and talking about Turkish democracy on a red carpet.

Inside a spacious conference room, I saw strings of bulbs hanging from the ceiling like theatre marquee lighting. A tall, tattooed man gazed pensively at the glass before him.

"This is Mario," said the headhuntress. "He's Italian and he's hot. We've brought him in yesterday." →

→    Well-versed in the antics of Giorgia Meloni, the YouTuber possessed an "uncanny sensitivity" about the kind of content that risked upsetting "the Italian prime minister, the Pope or any lay member of the Catholic Church." Poor Mario became an excommunicado a year prior after he had dissed "Catholic enemies of abortion" and defended "LGBTQI rights for nuns and priests" on his channel. Thousands of insults, written in perfetto Italiano, filled the comments section.

Italian fascists, he said, were grammar Nazis.

After I was seated, the headhuntress opened the translucent doors to reveal fresh brainpower. A turbaned journalist named Bashir described, in an agonised voice, what Narendra Modi had been doing to his fellow Kashmiris for the past few years. The far-right in India "idolised Valley bros, particularly Elon Musk," Bashir said. He confessed to feeling somewhat guilty about working in their Sacred Valley as a sensitivity reader.

I looked at the floor design embellished with crimson accents reminiscent of the company's color palette. There was a piece of paper right in front of me. It was inscribed with the company's letterhead that sat atop a phrase in all caps: SENSE AND SENSIBILITY

\* \* \*

Just as I stooped to pick it up, Hülya, a glamorous young woman in Louboutins, ente red the office. She said she was a runaway Saudi princess (no, not that one). Although her father, who ran a minuscule Gulf emirate, strongly opposed the idea, she had TikToked her way through life, documenting restrictions on things like female driving, female boozing and female laughing. "I'll tell you what my dad hates," said Hülya, "so you know what you shouldn't depict in this series."

Finally, Mo, a Chinese dissident, entered. He was the one I admired the most. The mild-spoken man, a blogger, has posted such insulting texts concerning the Chinese Communist Party (… while absurd and cruel, the reign of Maoists was not as fantastical as today's reign of Winnie the Pooh…) that he was presented with a choice of imprisonment or exile. Mo chose the latter and now lived in downtown LA, next to a go-go bar.

The headhuntress said sensitivity readers would join us from all around the world who'd

"Sense and Sensitivity will be the first film on earth that will disturb nobody," announced the official Instagram account days after the film went into production

partake in our deliberations via Zoom. We'd be part of an effort to produce "a global event" that would attempt to garner "higher ratings than Bridgerton". ("Fuck off!" said my wife, who found the idea preposterous.)

Actors from around the world would star in our four-hour long mini-series tentatively titled Sense and Sensitivity. Famed actors in numerous countries would speak in different tongues and display their national customs, making sure everyone (your mother, your spouse, your child, your grandmother, your lover—and you, too!) was hooked. The production aimed, said the headhuntress, that our "inclusionary, all-inclusive content" would "disturb not one soul on our wretched earth" and prove "addictive for its lack of offence, rather than its engagement with hateful themes and 'high street subjects.'"

\* \* \*

Every day, we censored. Crossed-out. Cancelled.

We censored a homoerotic peephole scene between a Bangladeshi boy and a Bangladeshi boy. We crossed out an extended French kissing scene between two step-sisters. We cancelled a whole character, the Third-wave Feminist Football Coach, for his radical views that might anger MAGA people. We learned that even the deplorable people had rights and dignity (and subscriptions to our service).

We were ruthless in our censorship: iconoclasts, progressives and the woke crowd tasted our red pen relentlessly. We ensured the most conservative people in any given society received the royal treatment and were not bothered by any annoyingly offensive detail. There wouldn't be a single complaint: you could be the most sensitive person on earth, yet nothing would offend you in our "content". "Zero," the headhuntress repeated each day. "Zero-disturbed is our motto. Equity in censorship! Hurray! How about a fresh round of kombuchas?"

We made sure people didn't smoke in Sense and Sensitivity. We ensured no discriminatory language was used against women in headscarves. We enforced a strict ban on antisemitic ➔

→ insinuations. Nobody made fun of others, even if they were funny. Nobody smoked, snuggled or snorted. The four-episode series would annoy no one, critique nothing and "rattle zero feathers."

Every morning, the headhuntress carried us fresh coffee, stacks of donuts and data reports on themes and words that angered subscribers the most. Snitch™, a new feature of the streaming app, allowed users to inform the company about an insulting phrase that had slipped through the net.

Marketing walked in tandem with us. "Sense and Sensitivity will be the first film on earth that will disturb nobody," announced the official Instagram account days after the film went into production. "Both your mad uncle and your gender-fluid children will dig it." Snitch™ reports of previous productions taught us exactly how to achieve that goal. I saw the company's new ad inside SFO's Harvey Milk Terminal: "Content doesn't need to be nasty to be tasty. Subscribe today and #exerciseyourrightnottobeoffended."

I gained 10 pounds during my time at that red office. A cup of Joe and donuts each hour added up. "I'm exercising my right not to exercise," I joked to my wife. Emotionally and philosophically, I felt emptied.

\* \* \*

We configured, censored and cancelled even as the shoot began.

We watched rushes and changed garments, taking issue with the length of a character's skirt (my grandmother would hate that!) and the colour of a blouse (green, the colour of Sharia, could give offence if worn by a sexy secretary). We opposed that reference to Winnie the Pooh in a scene where the protagonist tucks in with a Teddy Bear (Xi Jinping's trolls will hack our servers in no time). Our American lead, the guy who starred in Ferrari, was barred from speaking in an Italian accent (hello! Cultural Appropriation 101!). He ended up mouthing words precisely as he did in Girls: in Brooklynite English.

We intervened in music, too. The Billie Eilish song the millennial Muslim character streamed in the pilot episode (I could eat that girl for lunch /

Yeah, she dances on my tongue) had to go.

Hülya: My dad would chop my head off if I sang the line in his presecnce 'I could eat that girl for lunch'.

Mo: The tongue thing can also be considered, in mainland China, as a devious way of demanding cultural and linguistic rights for the Uyghur people.

The company had paid a few hundred million bucks to use the Eilish song. But giving offence would be more costly (population of China, 1.412 billion in 2022; GDP in UAE, US$509 billion in 2023).

Weeks passed. My inky fingers were a palimpsest of sensitivities breached. I'd look at my soft pink hands while lounging on the chaise lounge chairs on our terrace as the sun set, wondering at their immense powers to kill creativity and bring profits.

I knew which straw would break the camel's back in the Middle East. I learned how to dampen a character's refreshing, beautiful, severe tone. My inky fingers made things dull and unchallenging. A slight irritation with a proposed scene was enough for me to throw it back to its source. The scriptwriters, paid handsomely for their imaginative faculties, had to develop something better, something more sensitive to please my wounded mind.

Was I born to censor? Reader, no. I was just born sensitive.

\* \* \*

The date of the Sense and Sensitivity gala approached. A whole year had passed since my headhunting. My wife, who discussed the Black legacies of Marxism with her students during the week, said this was the only time we'd dress up during our stay in California. I placed an order at **GenerationTux.com**.

The gala would be held at Pantages, one of the great landmarks of Hollywood. The road trip was fun, although we weren't driven there in limos but in a ZipCar Prius. At the theatre, dignitaries worldwide were treated to caviar and California Chardonnay. I got drunk pretty quickly.

An hour later, I spotted Turkey's Minister of

Information and Combatting Fake News in the buffet queue. The real censors of the world had arrived to preview our sensitive content.

I noticed state dignitaries from China, Russia, Pakistan, Hungary, Poland and North Korea. I joined Mario, Hülya and Mo as they visited each group of guests, hearing their expectations from Sense and Sensitivity.

We were seated next to the Turkish minister and his wife, a bloated blonde who loved lobsters and worked as an apparatchik of the Turkish regime to afford them. There were tears in the couple's eyes as the film's protagonist, the guy from Girls, lost his beloved (a headscarved Turkish girl) at the finale in the fourth episode. They applauded vehemently before the Minister turned to me as the lights turned back on.

"See, you can make a great film without insulting Turkishness or our Supreme Leader," he grumbled. "Had you not stabbed us in the back so frequently in the past, you could have been writing a similar production for the company's Turkish channel, which I oversee."

Our film was sleek, and its characters were colourful, articulate and weird. It wasn't a conservative film by any stretch of the definition. The innocent marriage plot, set in our fragile, over-sensitive age, wouldn't look out of place in the Regency Era. A feel-good film that could harm or offend no one. We drove home a little after midnight and invoiced the company for the journey.

\* \* \*

Then the reviews were in.

All our tomatoes were rotten.

Critics, left, right and centre destroyed us.

"Did ChatGPT 1.0 come up with this?" asked The Guardian's esteemed critic. "This frictionless, superficial popsicle of a film works diligently to say nothing about our world. It melts into sugary, non-nutritious nonexistence with dizzying speed."

Ouch. Imagine how Anthony Lane would pan us in the New Yorker's new number.

The audience reaction was harsher.

"this seems engineered to gaslight viewers & really GETS ON MY NERVES by veiling all the stuff that MIGHT GET ON ANYONE'S NERVES!!!" someone tweeted.

"Lacks a heartbeat," said another. "So grey & boring & feels like John Major in film form." It seemed they'd instead stream an equivalent of Margaret Thatcher or Jeremy Corbyn.

Where were the bad feminists? Where were the smoking classes? Where were the risqué skirts? Where were the troubled Islamists who wanted to emigrate to Belgium and then blow up a charcuterie? Where were the skinheads who were both queer and fascist?

What had happened to the annoying ones? The pains in the ass? The swearers. The rumblers. What had happened to the ugly ones? The ones that spoke like they received no formal education in life? The ones who picked their noses?

In caring so much about the sensitivities of some, we had offended the taste and the good sense of the sensible. The Monday after the global release of Sense and Sensitivity, the company fired all its sensitivity readers. Its stock was down 31%.

On a breezy day in June 2024, my phone started ringing as we walked on the Santa Cruz beach. The headhuntress, who fired me a few weeks back, was planning to visit Bodrum for a Mediterranean fortnight. Did I have any recommendations for her? I paused a moment. My wife stared at me in anticipation. ("Will they now hire you as a travel agent?" she asked afterward.)

Sure, I said, I do have some tips for you. Drink a lot when you get to Turkey. Meet strangers who look like you won't get along with at all. Swim naked. Smoke a pack a day. Say something foulmouthed about the horrible people who exist on our earth. Annoy your hotel neighbours. Belly-dance. Break a law or two. Insult a public figure in a private conversation.

Lose it. Find it again. Shout and disturb and live a little. ✖

*Kaya Genç is Index's Turkey contributing editor and author of The Lion and the Nightingale: A Journey Through Modern Turkey, published by Bloomsbury*

53(02):99/103|DOI:10.1177/03064220241274945

# The unstilled voice
# of Gazan theatre

**LAURA SILVIA BATTAGLIA** recalls the last play she saw in
Gaza and talks to its director today about how theatre is still
providing a voice for the displaced, even in refugee camps

THEY EMERGE VERY slowly from a black hole in the background. Men and women, their faces tired, all take heavy steps. Some are dragging a bag, others have mattresses and household objects. The stage is lit in green and red, illuminating the young actors and dancers one by one, emphasising their individual suffering. The music - rapper Hijazi's remix of the traditional Palestinian choral song *Tarweeda Shamaly* - repeats in a hypnotic loop to tell us that, for 70 years, the story of Palestinians has always been the same: moving forward in an exhausting and constantly uprooting process. The Palestinians call it *Nakba* and this dance-theatre show named The Story is Sick by the Ayyam al Masrah company, the only one active in the strip, was performed just over a year ago live in Gaza. It was a performance like no other which I saw on a reporting mission to the strip. Today it seems to rise again in tragic reality, after 7 October 2023.

The theatre has been destroyed now and no longer exists. The cast and crew have paid a horrific price for living in Gaza. Of the company's 20 or so actors, aged between 20 and 35, many are displaced in Deir al-Balah. Only one, the stage technician, Ahmad Gheidar, decided to stay in Gaza, risking his life; a couple of actors, Mohannad and Lina, got engaged, left Gaza and did everything they could to escape to Egypt; three have died with all their families. None of the members of the company have a home to return to; their houses are all destroyed. The only thing left to the actors of Ayyam al Masrah is theatre, as the artistic director of the company, Mohammed al-Hessi recalls, constantly disturbed in the background by the buzz of Israeli drones.

For al-Hessi himself it was unimaginable that one of the play's ➜

LEFT AND OVERLEAF: A performance Battaglia saw in Gaza, before the theatre was destroyed

→ characters - a Palestinian, forced to abandon his home in 1967 and wander through refugee camps in the region – would be his reality a year later. Displaced from Gaza City after the Israeli bombings of November 2023, he and his wife and three daughters are searching for a fourth refuge, after Khan Younis, Deir al-Balah and Rafah.

"I am very worried," he told Index in a series of daily voice messages that continue a dialogue that has already lasted more than six months. "There are thousands of people who continue to move by cars and donkeys like us. After being shot in the back and miraculously unharmed, I spent two months on Rafah beach in al-Mawasi. Here, at times I hoped to end it all. The cold in February was excessive and we tried to survive by somehow diluting the salty sea water for drinking. I was morally destroyed

# None of the members of the company have a home to return to: their houses are all destroyed

by the impossibility of giving a dignified life to my wife and my daughters, but I didn't believe I would be forced to move again and again to get away from the bombings that reached us as far as the south of the strip".

Al-Hessi's fate is also that of a man unafraid to speak truth to power: inconvenient for Israel, to the point of not being able to leave Gaza for seven years now, because he raises political issues in his plays and is not afraid to highlight the impact of the Israeli occupation on Gazans' daily life; inconvenient for Hamas because the theatre company has

been the only one on the strip since 1995 that does not bow to the local powers that be. He has challenged Hamas's moral police by putting men and women on stage as couples and has had the courage to question the Islamic values on which daily life is based, stimulating debate among spectators. In the audience, men and women sit together, next to each other, condemned by Hamas authorities as a dangerous potential for "promiscuity".

In Gaza City, the success of The Story is Sick was so overwhelming when it was first staged in February 2023 that the

number of performances was doubled to 40. "People loved our show because it manages to generate a great debate between the public and the actors," al-Hessi told Index proudly. "After the performance everyone asks questions, as if looking for a solution. And the theatre has always been full: those who saw the show brought other people, students, associates. At the debut there were 350 people in the room and there were people waiting outside, sitting on the stairs."

For those who attended the play last spring, the atmosphere was alive with debate, pulsating even. From the stands, many were wondering about the weight of tradition on family relationships and how the Israeli occupation and segregated life on the Gaza strip made the patriarchal system and male-female dynamics more burdensome and complicated.

Hana Abd al-Nabi, a lively and dynamic actor in the company, wrote the script of The Story is Sick together with the artistic director. She explained: "In this show we faced a new challenge: it was the first year in which we added male figures to the narrators on stage because we had always entrusted the role of the narrator to a female voice and body. The audience so far had not been mixed but was mostly female only.

"We then inserted male characters into the show and encouraged the presence of young men in both to change their point of view on the topics treated in our comedies. The female character tells the story from her point of view, and the male character tells the same story from his point of view. As an author I had to split between genders: if I were a man, would my wife say a certain thing, and would she complain in a certain way? And what would I do if I were a woman? And who would be right

between the two? On stage, with respect to individual stories, both genders - man and woman - are right, each from their point of view. Actually, we still find ourselves trapped in the same cultural and social pattern, from the era of the Arabian Nights to the era of social media, where our entire lives, even private, are discovered, exhibited."

The project started with a workshop between 23 actors to understand how to tell a story. The cast of Ayyam al Masrah had gathered the voices of three generations of Palestinians from Jaffa, Haifa and all of historic Palestine. Stories of the first Intifada, the second, and life today. Stories of couples who got married or who lived together or who had a love story. Each actor brought six stories. "In this journey," said al-Hessi, "we saw something happen in front of us: in this story of the Palestinian people there was something sick. From 1948 to today, love and life have progressively disappeared. And we saw that the future in the eyes of the young was already broken, and

that each of us was torn to pieces. We saw how each event - an intifada, an offensive, a siege - had an increasingly worse effect on social life. In the difficulties of everyday life, in looking for a job, in family life: even love stories have disappeared."

The only moment al-Hessi smiles is when he talks about his workshops in refugee camps: "Our first show in 1995 was called Mothers. 200 women came to see it, and a long discussion started there too. Instead of an hour we stayed there for three hours because all the women wanted to talk. From there we started our storytelling programme for women. Now I have built a 20-minute show that stages our displacement in which women are once again the main characters and we will have three female actors on the stage. And I wrote another script, and I have three male actors on stage: it is a show tailored to the needs of children up to 12 years of age."

Al-Hessi's recipe is simple. At the end of the day, his bread is life: tragic, absurd, unexpected, constantly balanced between the grimace of pain and the laughter of survival. ✖

*Laura Silvia Battaglia is a journalist, filmmaker and radio-host based in Italy*

53(02):104/107|DOI:10.1177/03064220241270335

In the difficulties of everyday life, in looking for a job, in family life: even love stories have disappeared

PICTURED: The story of Achamma centres around a nun who has deviated from the holy path

# Silent order

The lives of nuns are at the centre of a string of bans in southern India, write **FUJEENA ABDUL KADER** and **UPENDER GUNDALA**, as they introduce a new translation of the work of author **VALLACHIRA MADHAVAN**

WHEN ROMAN CATHOLIC groups in Kerala called for the play *Kakkukali* (Hopscotch) to be banned in March 2023, it was merely the latest event in a pattern of censorship around works set in convents. The play explores the problems faced by a young nun, and after groups attempted to disrupt its staging, the Kerala Catholic Bishop Council requested a ban from the state government.

Francis Noronha, the author whose short story *Kakkukali* was based on, resigned from his government position in response to the controversy surrounding both this and his novel Masterpiece.

In another censorship attempt on the same theme in 1986, dramatist PM Antony's play *Christhuvinte Aaram Thirumurivu* (The Sixth Sacred Wound of Christ) sparked controversy, with Christian groups' demands prompting its prohibition.

This pattern of bans goes back almost as far as the inception of the state of Kerala itself, starting with a furore surrounding author Vallachira Madhavan's work.

Below is a translated extract from the book which caused so much controversy – in English for the first time.

Madhavan's 1960 novel Achamma is regarded as an important piece of Malayalam language literature, exposing the atrocities faced by a Catholic nun in a convent. It is considered to be the first prohibited book in Kerala after the country's establishment in 1957, eliciting strong protest from the regional Catholic pontificate and its fervent supporters.

Achamma's story unfolds as a moving and tragic portrayal of a nun who deviates from the intended holy path to embrace the harsh reality of street life, eventually leading to her death as a prostitute. Madhavan's nephew, film critic Aravindan Vallachira, said that an ex-nun once confessed to Madhavan about the horrors she confronted in a convent, which made her run away and become a prostitute.

The novel's 1963 ban, orchestrated by cabinet minister Pulloli Thomas Chacko, demonstrated the Church's powerful influence. Since Kerala's inception, the Church has played a prominent role in its politics, and the Catholic community provides a crucial voting bloc. This authority has traditionally been used to protect the Church's interests, even if it means silencing dissenting voices such as Madhavan's. Achamma comes from a poor Christian household facing financial and societal hardships. The story takes a devastating turn when her lover dies, leaving her with only one way to console her devastated parents – becoming a nun. The novel criticises institutionalised conventions that force financially disadvantaged women into the limited life of a nun, focusing on the coercive dynamics and challenges they endure. Despite being outlawed, it remains a daring literary work that addresses religious and societal issues that remain prevalent today.

Sebastian Adayantharath, the Syro-Malabar Catholic bishop, observed to the Economic Times (of India) that the influx of low-income nuns in Kerala peaked in the mid-1960s, a period coinciding with the publication of Achamma. Young women from economically-destitute households frequently chose a life in the convent, seeing it as a way to relieve the substantial financial pressures on their families.

During the 1960s and 1970s, it was common practice for destitute Christian families to commit one or two children to the Church, and allegations were made that parents were coercing their daughters into convent life. Moreover, difficulties such as male dominance and a lack of democracy frequently contributed to the distress endured by the nuns within the convent.

In parallel, the brave autobiographies of two nuns, Sister Jesme and Sister Lucy Kalapura – the 2009 book Amen: The Autobiography of a Nun, and 2019's In the Name of God, respectively – amplify the voices of those speaking up about the atrocities committed against nuns, revealing the disturbing reality of sexual abuse within convents.

Jesme's dismissal from the community was caused by authorities attempting to label her as mad, whilst Kalapura's expulsion was caused by her support for five nuns protesting against Franco Mulakkal, the Bishop of Jalandhar who was accused of raping a nun 13 times. There was widespread outrage when he was acquitted in 2022.

Kalapura continues to fight for her

position as a nun and, in the face of attempts to restrict their autobiographies, these courageous sisters use social media platforms to freely express their concerns, contributing to the ongoing discussion about the issues that plague convents.

Achamma's prohibition, which stemmed from unease with the representation of a nun's unusual path and lesbian relationships, reflects broader societal taboos and the Church's reluctance to address internal difficulties. At the moment, the region is dealing with the stark realities of unnatural deaths among nuns and the long search for justice.

Data collected by scholars Madona Mathew and P Vishnuprasad shows that the bodies of at least 17 nuns were discovered in various convents between 1987 and 2020, emphasising the urgent need for transparency and accountability. Many cases were promptly shut down by the authorities, who attributed them to suicides after conducting flimsy investigations.

In 2022, the life sentences given to a Catholic priest and a nun convicted of the murder of Sister Abhaya were suspended, and they were granted bail while they appealed. This case highlights the ongoing difficulties in confronting clerical sexual abuse. Sister Abhaya's body was found in a convent well in 1992, and her death sparked a 28-year investigation to find those responsible. Despite the enormity of the sexual abuse problem concerning priests, the Church remains unwilling to look into the matter internally.

In the midst of these pressing issues, the banned Achamma is all the more significant. It is a mirror reflecting societal and institutional barriers.

The 1963 ban on Madhavan's work did not prevent him from continuing his writing career. The following year, he published two novels through the Champakulam-based Bishop Kurialachery Memorial Book Depot. Perhaps surprisingly, this was a Catholic business venture named

# Allegations developed that parents were coercing their daughters into convent life

after Saint Thomas Kurialacherry of Champakulam.

The flood of letters from admirers during the 1960s and 1970s, all addressed simply to "Vallachira Madhavan, Thrissur, P.O., Kerala" with no home address, demonstrated the widespread audience he had there.

As a pioneer in the painkili sahityam (Malayalam popular literature) genre, he was instrumental in making literature more accessible to the general public.

But despite its popularity, this genre was heavily criticised. Madhavan's works prioritised everyday human experiences, resonating with the average literate Malayali reader rather than catering to the intellectual elite. Even today, prominent scholars argue that his works do not constitute "serious literature", and some told Index as much.

Some of Madhavan's publications are on the government's list of books for school libraries. But his books are not widely read or studied today, leaving him noticeably absent from the literary world. Why, despite being a prominent writer during his time, does Madhavan appear to have vanished from Kerala's literary history?

According to an official from the Sahitya Akademi in Thrissur, Madhavan's association with the Thattan (a group of goldsmiths) and what the Indian government officially terms "other backward classes" may have lessened his prominence. Despite being a popular author and the editor of a few journals, he struggled financially. →

→   Writer KV Ashtamoorthi recalls being asked by Madhavan, unrecognisable due to his worn and aged appearance, for a small sum of money. He said that accusations that Madhavan was a pornographic writer and that his works were indecent only added to the difficulties surrounding

his literary reputation until his death in 2013.Achamma's censors have almost succeeded in erasing his work. This makes it all the more important that we publish this extract, in English for the first time.

*Fujeena Abdul Kader is a doctoral fellow*

*at the National Institute of Technology, Rourkela, India. Her area of research is Literary Censorship and Controversial Literatures of India*

**Upender Gundala** *is assistant professor in literature at the National Institute of Technology, Rourkela*

# Achamma

### by Vallachira Madhavan

WHY DID ACHAMMA choose the path of a nun? As grief and desire intertwined with her bare thoughts in the evenings, Achamma pondered this question. It appeared to her as a deliberate choice, a selection of a form and emotion shrouded in profound silence.

Within the precincts of the monastery, all lamps were extinguished, and Achamma lay awake in the dead of night. Through the lattice window, she peered beyond, catching a glimpse of the world bathed in the moonlight's serenity. Achamma lay on the bed, staring at the southern part of the convent, the graveyard of maidens, where their temporal journeys concluded.

Amidst such observations, a shadow traversed the tableau of those lifeless maidens. Achamma saw a feminine form walking towards a grave beside the fence, standing atop the grave. Meanwhile, another figure emerged from outside the wall. It was a masculine figure. They united in a funereal embrace. Who were they? Achamma held her breath, absorbing the spectacle without intruding.

In the intertwining shadows, Achamma observed the enigmatic dance of darkness, the masculine form in the grasp of the feminine silhouette. With caution, she drew him closer, entwining the fingers of her androgynous form with his. Subsequently, as the two shadows descended between two graves, Achamma firmly shut the lattice window.

In Jasinda's room, Achamma heard her speaking to someone in a faint voice. It was an intimate exchange.

"Chew on a clove, it can help freshen up your stinking breath."

Achamma plugged her ears with her fingers and closed her eyes firmly. Suddenly, someone was knocking on her door. She restrained herself, anticipating who it could be. Removing her fingers, she concentrated. Someone was knocking.

Achamma moved the door latch and surrendered to the unknown force. Convinced of the inevitability, she followed it by closing her door from outside.

As another door opened, the clock chimed twice. Moments transpired, and the scene unfolded. "Jesus!" A voice echoed. Susie, Clara, Mary, Jasinda, Leelama... everyone heard. Each contemplated, unable to identify the voice. Who is screaming? Why?

But they are sure the source of the scream is the Mother Superior's chamber! No one dared to ask a question. Breaths and heartbeats heightened. No one moved. The silence persisted and appeared to last an eternity.

The door swung open abruptly in Mother Superior's room, with a muffled noise and a blend of footsteps rushing to the courtyard. Achamma ran away, screaming, "Jesus ... Jesus!" leaving the convent behind and the echoes of uncertainty.

Leelama rose and lit a candle to pray. There was the sound of Mother Superior's room door closing again. ✖

*Translated by Fujeena Abdul Kader and Upender Gundala*

53(02):108/110|DOI:10.1177/03064220241270339

LAST WORD

# Freedom of expression is the canary in the coalmine

Outgoing Index chief executive **RUTH ANDERSON**, who is making a return to full-time politics, reflects with **MARK STIMPSON** on the past four years

RUTH ANDERSON JOINED Index on Censorship as its chief executive at one of the strangest times in recent memory.

"I started during the pandemic when authoritarian regimes used the pretext of Covid-19 as an excuse to restrict access to a free media," she said.

Anderson was born in Edinburgh, the daughter of a Scottish trade unionist. Her mother is from east London, her family having arrived there during the 1890s, fleeing the pogroms in Russia.

Anderson took politics and international relations at the University of Birmingham.

She was elected to the UK parliament as Labour MP for Stoke-on-Trent North in 2015, losing her seat in the Conservative party's successful attack on the so-called Red Wall in the 2019 election.

In late 2022, she was granted a life peerage as Baroness Anderson of Stoke-on-Trent.

She recognises that being CEO of Index is to act as a "temporary custodian" of an organisation that has striven to protect freedom of censorship for more than 50 years.

"When the uninitiated ask about Index, I tell them that our origins could have come from one of Graham Greene's novels – and he was an early supporter," she said.

"Our story is one initiated at the height of the Cold War, with tales of *samizdat*, political dissidents, tyrants and, of course, more than the odd dose of unimaginable bravery."

"Today, Index is a proud and determined NGO, which speaks truth to power without fear or favour."

In the four years that followed her arrival, Anderson's in-tray was never empty.

"Putin invaded Ukraine (again) and sought to destroy a culture as well as a people. The people of Afghanistan were abandoned to the Taliban – with women who had fought so hard for their rights to freedom of expression left to vicious and dogmatic censorship. And a more aggressive Chinese Communist Party moved daily against dissent both at home and abroad – with a vivid showcase of their repression on show in Hong Kong. And this is before I mention Mexico, Belarus, North Korea, Myanmar or even Iran."

Anderson is handing over custodianship of Index to former editor-in-chief, Jemimah Steinfeld, so it seemed like the opportune moment to interview her for our Last Word column.

**MARK STIMPSON** What was your first memory of realising that not everyone has freedom of expression?

**RUTH ANDERSON** I have a vivid memory of my mum singing a protest song about Nelson Mandela when I was a very young child. I inevitably asked who he was. This was my first exposure to the reality of political prisoners and the bravery of dissidents.

**MS** What took you into politics?

**RA** I come from a family of extraordinary women. Every week my grandmother's friends would bring their post to her flat and she would help them reply to their letters. She was lucky to be more literate. My mum helped people at work, day-in-day-out, fighting for their rights and incomes. These amazing women instilled in me the responsibility to help those people who need it, when they need it.

Too often the status quo doesn't work, and those with louder voices can help change the world.

**MS** What aspect of Index's work has been most interesting to you?

**RA** Our values are more than words on a page. Our core rights need to be celebrated, cherished and protected. The right to freedom of expression is the canary in the coal mine – when regimes seek to restrict speech and undermine protest, it demonstrates their fear of their people. The bravery of those who will speak truth to power must never be underestimated, which is why I was so proud to lead Index.

**MS** What do you think Index's greatest achievement was during your tenure? →

## Index's story is one initiated at the height of the Cold War

CREDIT: Chris McAndrew

**→ RA** The team at Index have done extraordinary work over the last four years. Our work on Slapps has been world-leading, our journalism has thrived, our magazine is beautiful and a great read. I'm really proud of what we have achieved, but the greatest achievement has been providing a platform for dissidents and re-establishing Index's voice at the heart of the fight for global freedom of expression.

**MS** Do you think you will still champion freedom of expression in the House of Lords?

**RA** As a given!

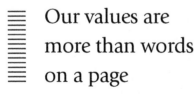

## Our values are more than words on a page

**MS** If you were detained and could take one book to jail with you, what would it be?

**RA** This is probably the hardest question to answer. I love the written word so I'll need to cheat! Can I have the collected works of Robert Caro? His four volume biography of Lyndon B Johnson is one hell of a read and would keep me going for months.

**MS** What piece of art has moved you the most?

**RA** The Holocaust Memorial on Miami Beach.

**MS** What news headline would you most like to read?

**RA** Hmmm… Just one? Can I have three? "UK Labour Landslide." "Israel and the Palestinians sign peace agreement and agree terms for a

ABOVE: Baroness Anderson is sworn in to the House of Lords

two-state solution."
"Putin's forces leave Ukraine."

**MS** Last thoughts as you become a government whip in the House of Lords?

**RA** It would be remiss of me not to thank my amazing chair, Trevor Phillips, and our brilliant board of trustees. With me, they've helped Index rebrand, relaunch and celebrate our 50th birthday. They've rebuilt the organisation into the force I believe it to be. Their commitment to Index has been unwavering and without them Index wouldn't be here today. A final word to Index's new CEO: Jemimah, you know how special Index is, and under your stewardship we are going to go from strength to strength. ✖

CREDIT: Parliament Live

53(02):111/112|DOI:10.1177/03064220241271526

# Subscribe

An archive of past battles won, and a beacon for present and future struggles.

Times Literary Supplement

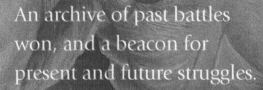

**Annual print subscription***
£40 / $75

**Index on Censorship iOS app**
A 30-day subscription for £1.49

**Single print issue****
£13 / $24

**Annual digital subscription**
£17.99

**Single digital issue**
£5.99

We believe in independent reporting around the world. We have contributing editors and correspondents filing from Mexico, China, South Korea, the USA, Italy, Yemen, Iraq and Turkey. We always pay our writers so they can carry on their work. Support us and support independent journalism.

*Annual subscription includes 4 issues. **Single issues available on Amazon. For print subscriptions, email subscriptions@sagepub.co.uk or call: +44 (0)20 7342 8701. For digital subscriptions, visit: exacteditions.com/indexoncensorship. Exact Editions app available on iPad, iPhone and Android and includes access to 38 archive issues

### indexoncensorship.org
Index on Censorship is published quarterly in April, June, September and December by Sage (Los Angeles, London, New Delhi, Singapore, Washington DC and Melbourne).
   Annual subscription (2023) including postage: institutional rate (combined print and electronic) £466/US$861; individual rate (print only) £35/US$65. Electronic only and print only subscriptions are available for institutions at a discounted rate. Note VAT is applicable at the appropriate local rate.

For the full range of institutional / individual subscriptions, single issue and back issue purchasing options visit indexoncensorship.org/subscribe. To activate your subscription (institutions only) visit online.sagepub.com.

Sage Publications Ltd, 1 Oliver's Yard, 55 City Road, London EC1Y 1SP, UK tel. +44 (0)20 7324 8500, fax +44 (0)20 7324 8600 and in North America, Sage Publications Inc, PO Box 5096, Thousand Oaks, CA 91359, USA.

Sage is a member of CrossRef.

Periodicals postage paid at Rahway, NJ. POSTMASTER, send address corrections to Index on Censorship, c/o Mercury Airfreight International Ltd, 365 Blair Road, Avenel, NJ 07001, USA.

### SUBMISSION GUIDELINES AND ADVERTISING
If you are interested in submitting a pitch for an article, please contact jemimah@indexoncensorship.org. We look for timely and original work – journalistic features and fiction – with a strong link to our theme of freedom of expression. Please send a short synopsis of your proposal and an author bio.

### COPYRIGHT
Sage and Writers and Scholars International require the author as the rights holder to sign a Journal Contributor's Publishing Agreement. In this agreement the author will be requested to grant Writers and Scholars International the sole and exclusive right to publish for 90 days from publication, followed by a non-exclusive licence to publish and sub-license the work for the full legal term of copyright.

   Disclaimer: To the extent permitted by law the authors, editors, publisher, and the Society (Writers and Scholars International Ltd) will not accept any legal responsibility for any errors or omissions that may be made in this publication. The publisher makes no warranty, express or implied, with respect to the material contained herein.

### ABSTRACTING AND INDEXING
Please visit ioc.sagepub.com and click on the Abstracting/Indexing link on the left hand side to view a full list of databases in which this journal is indexed.

© Writers and Scholars International, 2023.

Apart from fair dealing for the purposes of research or private study, or criticism or review, and only as permitted under the Copyright, Designs and Patent Act 1988, this publication may only be produced, stored or transmitted, in any form or by any means, with the prior permission in writing of the Publisher, or in the case of reprographic reproduction, in accordance with the terms of licences issued by the Copyright Licensing Agency, US.

   Authorisation to photocopy journal material must be obtained directly from Sage or through a licence from the Copyright Clearance Center, Inc. (copyright.com). Enquiries concerning reproduction outside those terms should be sent to jemimah@indexoncensorship.org

indexoncensorship.org/subscribe

ISSN 0306-4220 ( 202407 ) 53 : 2 : 1 - B

ISBN 978-1-0362-06567

# INDEX
## ON
# CENSORSHIP

A VOICE FOR THE PERSECUTED

🌐 indexoncensorship.org

𝕏 @indexcensorship

ⓕ @indexoncensorship

ⓘ @indexcensorship

Support Index at indexoncensorship.org/donate